THE ART JOURNAL WORKSHOP

QUARRY

First published in the United States of America by
Quarry Books, a member of
Quayside Publishing Group
100 Cummings Center
Suite 406-L
Beverly, Massachusetts 01915-6101
Telephone: (978) 282-9590
Fax: (978) 283-2742
www.quarrybooks.com
Visit www.Craftside.Typepad.com for a behind-the-scenes peek at our crafty world!

Library of Congress Cataloging-in-Publication Data
Bunkers, Traci.
    The art journal workshop : break through, explore, and make it your
own / Traci Bunkers.
       p. cm.
1. Handicraft. 2. Scrapbook journaling. I. Title.
    ISBN-13: 978-1-59253-684-9
    ISBN-10: 1-59253-684-0
TT157.B815 2011
745.593--dc22

                                                              2010040310
                                                                     CIP

Digital edition published in 2011
eISBN-13: 978-1-61058-018-2

10 9 8 7 6 5 4

Design: Nancy Ide Bradham, www.bradhamdesign.com
Photography: Glenn Scott Photography
Step Photography: Traci Bunkers
DVD: Cybergraphix, Inc.

Printed in China

THE ART JOURNAL WORKSHOP

BREAK THROUGH, EXPLORE, AND MAKE IT YOUR OWN

BEVERLY MASSACHUSETTS

QUARRY BOOKS

TRACI BUNKERS

CHAPTER 1:
Introduction to Visual Journaling

CHAPTER 2:
Materials

CHAPTER 3:
Working Details

CHAPTER 4:
Art Journaling Exercises

CHAPTER 1:

Many people want to express themselves through visual journaling but are intimidated or feel unable to get started. They aren't sure what to write or how to move beyond writing a few phrases, gluing down a few images, or putting some paint on the paper. They don't know what to do or more importantly, what to do next.

When I asked a fellow artist what she would like to learn about visual journaling, her reply was, "I don't know what to write! Or how to get a page ready for writing and have all the little objects such as photos or whatever to go along with the writing ... I feel like I just don't know what to do." Often people feel a strong desire to journal, but they don't know how to incorporate the different elements that will work as a whole.

Through my teaching and by speaking with people interested in visual journaling, I find that people get hung up on different things as they try to work, whether it's how to use an art supply to get the effect they want or more importantly, how to express what they want. They aren't interested in copying what someone else did or working in a cookie-cutter fashion. They want the tools and guidance to do it their way, in their style, creating work imbued with personal substance.

This book will be the next best thing to taking a workshop with me. I will help you to break through the surface for a deeper experience. Our focus here is the process and the journey of visual journaling, not the outcome. The finished page is a bonus; whether it's visually appealing or not isn't important. This book photographically illustrates the step-by-step process by which I work through each exercise and create a journal page. The enclosed DVD shows time-lapse photography of the entire process for several exercises. Although the goal is not for you to re-create the same

pages in the same way I did, this process will show you how to problem solve and avoid roadblocks that might keep you from getting to the inner personal work during your exploration of the exercises.

The beginning of the book discusses the various materials that can be used in visual journaling. It also suggests solutions for overcoming some common stumbling blocks. The real work starts with journaling prompts and exercises that range from playful to deep. There are three different kinds: "Journaling Prompts & Exercises", "Call to Action Exercises", and "Self-Care Exercises". Most of these are worked through in a book you choose to use as your art journal. These exercises can be worked in any order. Feel free to jump around and work on whatever sounds interesting. But keep in mind that the ones you are avoiding are often the ones you need to do the most!

AN IMPORTANT NOTE

I'm not a doctor or therapist nor do I play one on TV. I'm just a very introspective artist who is experienced in visual journaling and expressing myself. The process comes naturally for me, but I know that for most people, it doesn't. That's why I'm writing this book: to help you express yourself. While you are working through the exercises in this book, if feelings or issues come up that are too much for you to deal with on your own, please don't hesitate to seek professional help.

WHAT IS VISUAL JOURNALING?

Journaling conjures up thoughts of writing, but what exactly is visual journaling or an art journal? The terms are used loosely, so I'd like to talk about them. To some, an art journal, or visual journal, is simply an artist's book containing mixed-media work, such as collage and painting. To me, it's much more than that. My visual journals combine painting, photographs, collage, stamping, and writing from the heart. Combining words with visual imagery is much more powerful than either one alone. By combining the two, I create something that is fresh and rich in meaning sometimes raw, expressing hurt or pain, and sometimes elated, expressing immense joy. It's work I do for myself without looking for the approval of an audience or worrying what someone else might think. It's not the finished product that is important but the process that gets me there. I'm not trying to make art, I'm just taking a journey. I am open to where it takes me and to what happens in the process. Because of that, I leave my internal (and external) censors at the door. Busying my hands with collaging, painting, and stamping as I work frees up my mind, distracting it in a way. I am able to get out of my own way and freely express or process whatever I need or want to work on. Visual journaling stills the mind and silences the censors.

So back to the original question: What is visual journaling? It's personal expression using mixed media and writing in a visual, two-dimensional manner, usually in a book format. That brings us to the next question.

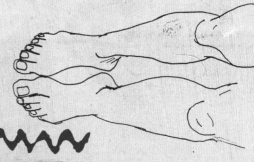

WHY DO IT?

Personally, I keep a visual journal because I'm emotional and I need to express myself and work out my feelings. It's extremely cathartic. It's a way for me to actively work through difficult experiences, issues, or patterns by getting it out on the page with paint and scribbles and photographs and words. Often while I'm working, because my hands are busy, my monkey mind stops and I have revelatory moments. A lightbulb goes on. It's also a way for me to deal with my chronic pain. But visual journaling isn't just about dealing with the dark side or shadow self; it's also a way to express passion, joy, and happiness.

If you're feeling in a funk, working in your journal is a fairly quick (and free) way to change your mood. It can energize and center you. You will feel calmer and more focused afterward. Journaling about something that's emotional or upsetting can sometimes be draining, but it can be necessary to help you to move through the issue or pain.

Some people don't want to put anything negative in their journal. But I feel that is censoring yourself and avoiding those feelings. It's also denying who you are and what you're feeling or going through. Dealing with those feelings or experiences in a journal is a positive way to gently begin to shine light on those areas in a safe, protected way. Remember, you're doing this for yourself, and no one else has to see it.

Your journal can be a visual documentation of your life experiences, both good and bad, along with your dreams, goals, and hopes. You can journal about everything, even painful things, because they all make up who you are and help you to become who you want to be. How cool is that? And it's all colorfully documented in a book. Not only is your journey a visual, creative personal expression, but you can look through it and see where you've been and how far you've come. Regardless of what it's about, whether it's painful or sad or over-the-top joy, it's all beautiful, even in the darkness, because it's you.

All this aside, I just love working in my journal and I hope you will too. It's a creative birthing process, and every time I work in my book, it's a new experience. I wish you the same fulfillment.

MATERIALS

CHAPTER 2:

Before I discuss the different materials you can use, I'd like to make an important point. This type of work can be done without any special materials or any special book. Chances are you already have some things you can use for the exercises or to create an art journal. The important point is to not let the materials (or lack of them) get in the way of creating. But with that said, I do recommend you get the best materials you can afford. I use a very wide variety of materials, ranging from dollar store and kids' craft items to higher-end paint or tools for writing. But generally, with certain materials, the quality is related to the cost. I love using inexpensive markers. But I also know they dry out much faster and aren't as vibrant as more expensive markers. The same goes for paints and inks. I use both craft store paints and higher-end paints. The higher-end paints have more pigment, which means they go farther and have richer colors. In some ways, you do get more bang for your buck, but spend what you can.

The materials discussed in this chapter are merely suggestions. I use them on a regular basis, so I'm familiar with them and they suit my style of work. Depending on your artistic slant, you might prefer different supplies. If you aren't sure what you like, play around with different materials to see what gives you the results you want. By watching the videos on the enclosed DVD, you can see how different materials are used and the effects they create. If you want to try something without making a large investment, start with an inexpensive version

of the item. Or just buy one or two of something, such as a particular marker you want to try, instead of getting a whole set. Then as you develop a feel for the materials that work best, you can invest in the higher-quality items or simply a larger quantity of what you like.

Also, if you don't have something you feel you need right away, there's always a solution. For example, if you don't have any adhesive and you want to glue down some pictures, just attach them with clear tape. Or if you don't have any gesso but need to tone down a printed page in your journal, cover it with masking tape. I frequently use tape as a fix-all in my work. If a collaged item won't stick, I put clear or decorative tape on it to hold the edges down.

THE JOURNAL

Choosing a Book

Choosing a book to use as an art journal is personal. Finding the book that is "just right" is important because the more you like your book, the more you will want to work in it. If something about it isn't quite right, then you won't be drawn to journal in it. Experience is really the only way to figure out what style of book you prefer. If you are new to journaling, you might want to choose a book that isn't too thick. That way if it's not perfect for you, you'll get through it quickly and can try something a little different next.

Here are some things to consider when choosing a book.

★ **Type:** There are many types of new and used books to choose from. Would you like to work in an old, used book, or something brand new and blank, or even handmade? Old books not only have a sense of history and a past life, they also already have printing and pictures on the pages. A journal page can be created so that bits and pieces of the original printing might peek out, adding to the visual texture. I am an avid recycler and like to use old books as a way of repurposing them. I get them from thrift stores, garage sales, and my local library's book sale. I either work directly in an old book or I take it apart and bind a new book, using its covers and putting in a mix of different pages. A blank book is also nice to use because you are giving it life, and nothing is already on the page to distract you. In the end, it's all a matter of personal preference.

★ **Binding:** Consider how a book is bound before deciding to use it. Don't worry if you know nothing about the different types of book bindings. What you need to evaluate is how flat the book lays when it's open. Books that don't lay flat are hard to work in. Spiral-bound books lay perfectly flat, and you can fold the pages together to work on one side of the book at a time. But you can't work across the middle. Some spiral-bound books are perforated on the pages near the binding. While this makes it easy to remove pages, it also means the wear and tear of working might pull them out. So consider one without perforations.

★ **Size:** Do you want a book small enough to throw in your bag to carry around with you? Or can it be big because you will keep it in your work area? Do you like to work small or sprawl out onto big pages? I like to work in books that are around 8" x 10" (20 x 25.5 cm), but I also like slightly smaller books, depending on what I'm using the journal for. For the exercises in this book, I recommend using a book that is at least 7" x 9" (18 x 23 cm) so there will be enough space to fully realize your ideas.

★ **Thickness:** If you like to work in the same book for a long time, you might choose a thick one. If you like the excitement of starting a new book regularly, a thin one might be better. If this is your first art journal, I suggest starting with a thinner book so the size isn't intimidating.

★ **Paper Weight:** Thin, brittle pages won't work that well. Pages need to hold up to the wetness of paints and glue. If they are too thin, they can be fortified with collage and also by applying a coat of gesso. But they need to be thick enough to hold up to either of those applications. Nothing is sadder than the pages in your journal falling apart, so choose a book with sturdy pages.

★ **Paper Finish:** Avoid books with glossy pages, because paint or gesso might just flake off instead of bonding to the paper. Glossy paper can also be difficult to write on with pens and markers. Matte pages or those with a soft gloss rather than a shiny surface will work fine.

Preparing the Book

No matter what type of book you use, chances are you will have to remove some of the pages. If you don't, your book might fall apart over time. Collaging and painting on the pages will make the book thicker. This thickness can break the spine or in the case of a spiral-bound book, make it difficult to turn the pages. I have found that most books need to have about a quarter to a third of the pages removed. If the top cover slants down from the spine to the opposite edge with the book on its back, enough pages have been removed.

If you are working in a book made specifically as an art journal, you might not need to remove any or as many pages.

Removing Pages from Books with Sewn Signatures

If you have a book with sewn-in signatures, you can simply tear out pages from the center of each signature, removing about a quarter to a third of each signature. A signature is a section of folded pages that are nested and stitched together in the binding process. Books are generally made up of multiple signatures. If you are using a printed book and don't want to remove the middle spread of a signature because you like the text or imagery, just go to the previous page and carefully tear it out while holding down its other half. Then the other half of the page will come out. Keep in mind that the pages will come out in pairs (the right and left sides of a folded page). So you might want to look at both sides to see if you want to keep or remove them.

For books made up of sewn signatures, the pages can be removed anywhere within a signature as long as a third to a quarter of each signature is removed. In other words, the book needs to have about the same number of pages removed from each signature so that the pages in the book are evenly distributed. Do not tear out an entire signature and leave another one intact. That will leave too much space in one area of the spine and not enough in another.

Handmade book showing slant from spine to fore edge

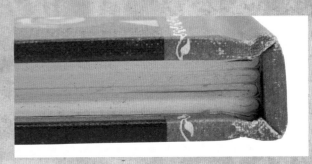

A book with four sewn signatures

ia, New Jersey and New York, tion's silk and rayon mills. years employment in the tex- off. From 1923 to 1927 some re employed, but in 1929 the to 1,100,000. A part of this he introduction of better tex- y more efficient ways of run- 931 there were only 850,000 ause of the nation-wide busi- our people bought less cloth- mber had risen to 1,080,000.

higher pay for skilled work, the stretch-out and speed-up tled with the help of the T Board appointed by Preside

In 1935, the Supreme Co unconstitutional, and the workers fell to as low as $7 a of the textile companies and ning cotton mills agreed to k of wages and hours. This v employees.

Many of the troubles of t

Exposed stitching in the middle of a signature

Removing pages from the middle of a signature

TIP Don't throw out the pages you removed! Save those to use for collage material either for working the journaling exercises or for other projects. That's the beauty of this type of art. You can always recycle and repurpose!

Old book with pages removed from the sewn signatures

If a book has sewn signatures, you will see small groupings of pages with a slight gap in the middle when looking at the top or bottom edge of the book. The gap is the middle of the signature. Open the book as close as possible to the middle of the first signature. Then turn pages until the stitching is visible in the middle. Tear out the desired amount of pages in each signature, being careful not to break the thread that holds the signature together.

Removing Pages from Spiral-Bound Books

It is very easy to remove pages from spiral-bound books. Simply tear them out and remove the narrow strip on the inside of the spiral. You can either remove the amount of pages necessary before you start or remove them as you work since each page is single and won't affect the other pages.

Removing Pages from Other Books

If your book isn't made up of a spiral binding or visibly sewn signatures, the pages can still easily be removed. Remove approximately a quarter to a third of the pages (about every third or fourth page) and keep the spacing of the removed pages fairly even throughout the book. If you like what's on the page to be removed, leave it in and take out the next.

Cutting pages from a book using a craft knife and cutting mat

Put a cutting mat under the page you want to remove, up against where it is attached at the spine. This protects the pages underneath. Then with a sharp craft knife, cut the length of the page, near where it is bound. Don't cut too close to the binding or its mate might fall out. Don't worry about cutting straight because it will likely get covered up with collage.

Instead of cutting the page, you can also tear against a steel ruler. Lay the ruler over the middle of the book with the right edge near the spine. While holding the ruler down, tear the page against it with the other hand. This leaves a narrow strip of the page attached to the book, making sure that its mate won't fall out. Remove pages throughout the entire book, and then check the slant to see if you need to remove more.

Removing a page by tearing it against a ruler

MISCELLANEOUS TOOLS

These items don't get the glory of juicy paints or markers, but they are still important.

Hair Dryer

A hair dryer allows you to quickly dry your work and continue working. I prefer a hair dryer over a heat gun because the extreme heat from a heat gun can be too hot for acrylic paints, adhesives, and glitter glues and will actually melt them instead of dry them.

Waxed Paper

Waxed paper can be used under the journal spread you are working on to protect the other pages. Place it on top of something you have just glued down before rolling over it with a brayer to keep adhesive from getting on the brayer or the rest of the page. It can also be used as a paint palette, under an item when applying glue, and to protect your work surface. An alternative is deli paper that is cut into folded sheets, making it is easy to pull it out of the box with one hand.

Brayer

A brayer is a printmaking tool with a handle and a roller. Use a brayer to ensure good contact between two pieces you're gluing together. It can also be used to apply paint.

Paint Palette

A paint palette is basically anything that holds paint for mixing or applying. I use a kids' plastic place mat from the dollar store. If you cut them in half, you have two smaller pieces that don't take up as much space. Clean the place mat with a baby wipe or with water. If the paint dries on a palette, it can usually be scraped off with a credit card. A glossy magazine, wax paper, or plastic lid can also be used.

Water Container

A water container is needed to hold water for rinsing paint brushes or for diluting paint. Anything that will hold water will work, as long as several brushes won't tip it over.

Sealant

It's good to seal some mediums such as water-soluble oil pastels or something that might transfer onto a facing page when the book is closed. Some people use gel medium as a sealant, but I prefer to use a workable fixative, which is a spray sealant. It seals the page, and you can still work on top of it after it's sealed. You can't do this with normal spray fixatives because they create a slick surface with nothing for the new materials to grab on to. It's better to apply a few light coats than one heavy one.

A variety of tools

Using a hair dryer to speed up the drying process

With waxed paper protecting the brayer from adhesive, a brayer is rolled over a collaged piece to ensure good adhesion.

TIP Workable fixative can be used to seal inkjet prints that aren't printed with waterproof ink so you can work on top of the print without the ink bleeding.

ADHESIVES

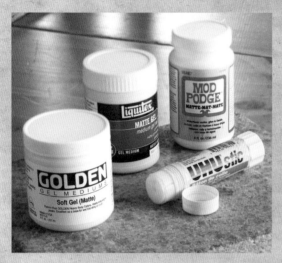

Adhesives, obviously, are used to glue items onto a page. If you plan to do a lot of layering with collage and paint, I recommend gel medium as a great all-purpose adhesive since what you glue down needs to be solidly adhered. If it's not, when you paint on top of it, it'll come up. It works best to apply the adhesive to the piece being collaged rather than applying it to the base.

Gel Medium

Gel medium is basically thick glue. Some brands of gel medium come in different consistencies, such as Golden's, which comes in soft, regular, and heavy, or Liquitex, which comes in regular, heavy, and super heavy. I recommend the consistency of the thinnest gel for collaging.

Mod Podge

While gel mediums are the top-of-the-line adhesive for collaging, the middle of the road is Mod Podge. It is thinner than gel medium and readily available in craft and hobby stores.

White Glue

Plain white glue can be too watery and cause wrinkling in the paper it's applied to, especially for larger items. Using a brush to spread it onto the item will help apply it evenly and cut down on the wrinkling.

Glue Sticks

If you're collaging something small that you know you won't be painting over, a glue stick will work fine, especially if it's applied thickly, like icing. But all glue sticks are not alike! I recommend Uhu glue sticks.

TIP Use a magazine for the background when applying glue. Lay the piece to be collaged facedown on the opened magazine and then apply the glue. After both pages of the magazine have been used this way, turn the page. This keeps glue from gelling onto the surface of the next piece to be collaged. When the magazine is all glued up, recycle it!

Applying adhesive with a brush to the back of an item, using a magazine as a protective background

CUTTING TOOLS

Most cutting mats are self-healing, so they can be used over and over again. They come in different sizes and usually have a measurement grid on them, making it easy to cut paper without having to first measure with a ruler.

Steel Ruler

A steel ruler can be used in two ways: as a guide for a craft knife to ensure a straight cut or as a guide to tear paper against for a straight but slightly deckled edge. I use this technique often to tear pages out of a book or to tear ephemera into smaller pieces. A steel ruler with a nonskid backing keeps the ruler in place while either cutting or tearing against it.

You will need cutting tools to cut out images, words, and anything else you might want to collage into your journal. You may also need them to remove some of the pages from your book, depending on how your book is bound. The main cutting tools for art journaling are basic scissors and a craft knife, but you can also use a steel ruler and a cutting mat along with them.

Scissors

Choose the size of scissors based on what you'll be cutting. I mainly use small, sharp scissors because it's easier to make small, controlled cuts with them. For cutting heavier items, like cardboard or chipboard, larger scissors are better.

Craft Knife and Cutting Mat

A craft knife and a cutting mat go hand in hand. You shouldn't use a craft knife to cut something on a table without a cutting mat underneath to protect the surface.

A craft knife is a small cutting tool with either replaceable blades or a blade that extends out and is snapped off in sections as it gets dull. Either type will work fine. Use a craft knife when more precise cuts are needed than you can get with scissors or for removing pages from your book. Always use a sharp blade to get a clean cut. A dull blade might tear the paper. Be sure to keep your fingers out of the way while cutting with a craft knife.

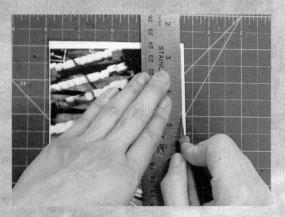

Cutting against a steel ruler with a craft knife for a straight edge

Tearing against a steel ruler to create a softer but straight edge

Using an awl to poke holes for inserting the brads

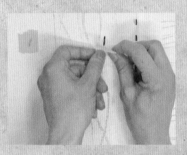

Inserting the brads through the holes to attach the piece to the journal page

Use masking tape to cover the legs of the brads on the back of the page. The backs of staples have already been covered to protect the page

ATTACHMENT TOOLS

Materials other than adhesives can both attach things into your journal and embellish. Often I use them solely to embellish because I like the way they look. Although it's not necessary, you can attach the item first to the page with an adhesive, and then use tape, brads, staples, or sewing not only for decoration, but to ensure the items are attached well.

TIP

Because I work in my book from front to back, I use only attachment techniques that go through both the item and the page on the right-hand page of my journal spread. Otherwise it might interfere with the artwork on the reverse side of the page. If I want brads or staples on the left page, I attach them only through the item itself and then glue it to the left page. I sew items onto a slightly bigger piece of paper and then glue that to the left page.

Brads and Staples

Brads and staples are a decorative way to attach or simply embellish an item. I use them when attaching tabs to the side of a journal page or in the corners of my photos. Both have come a long way from the standard selection in the office supply section. The scrapbook sections of craft stores offer all different shapes, sizes, and colors of brads. Staples now come in many colors and basically two sizes: standard and mini.

[How to Use It]

Make a hole where the brad will be attached with a needle or an awl. Place a cutting mat under the page to protect the pages underneath. Insert the legs of the brad through the hole and spread them apart on the other side of the page.

Stapling a photo solely for decoration

Tape

It's amazing how many different kinds of decorative tape can be found. Masking tape works great as a base to cover up the original printing on a page or anything else that needs to be covered. It takes acrylic paint well and gives an aged look. If something starts coming unglued as you're working, tape is a great solution, and it visually becomes part of the piece. Look for interesting tape at dollar stores, office supply stores, and hardware stores. Asian bookstores and Etsy.com have really lovely colored and patterned tape.

Sewing Supplies

Items can be hand-sewn onto the page, or stitching can be pure decoration. Any kind of thread, embroidery floss, or yarn can be used, as long as it can be threaded through a needle. Machine sewing is another option, either for sewing items together outside the journal or for decorative stitching on a surface. Stitched pieces can then be glued into the journal.

[How to Use It]

For hand-stitching: Cut thread about 24" (61 cm), thread it through a needle with an appropriately sized eye, and knot one end of the thread. A piece that is too long will get tangled. To make the knot show, start sewing on the right side. To hide the knot on the reverse side of the page, start from the wrong side. Sew around the piece as desired.

To make parallel bars of stitching, go down through the paper and come up with the needle so that the new hole is at an angle to the previous hole. Then go straight across and into the piece to make a new hole, coming back up at an angle. This will make parallel dashes on the right side and diagonal dashes on the wrong side.

To finish off, bring the needle through to the side where you want the knot and tail to be. Holding the needle flat against the paper, wrap the thread around it once, forming a tight loop. Hold your finger against the loop while pulling the needle through. Remember that any stitching will show on the reverse side of the paper. If it's not covered, the needle holes might allow paint or gesso to go through to the other side onto the page with the sewn piece. To protect the already-worked side, cover the stitching with collage, tape, or stickers before working on the other side.

Using tape to help hold down the edges of a thick instant photo

A photo hand-sewn to a journal page with the knots and thread tails exposed

Making a knot to securely finish off the sewing.

Sewing a photo onto a loose background paper with a sewing machine

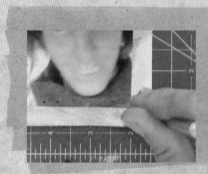

TIP If the piece you want to sew is thick, like a piece of cardboard or a photo from a photo lab, prepunching holes with an awl might make it easier to get the needle through.

A variety of items that can be used for embellishing

Embellishing a journal page with a rub-on

Glitter glue

Spreading glitter glue out with a brush after it's applied

EMBELLISHMENTS

Scrapbooking sections of craft stores have a vast array of embellishments that can be used in your journal pages. You probably already have some of these on hand.

Stickers

Keep an eye out for fun and odd stickers. There are many in the scrapbooking or kids' section of craft stores, in stationery stores, and in Asian bookstores. Check out ethnic stores in your area to see what you can find and don't forget the dollar store. Alphabet stickers are fun for spelling out words or to highlight one letter of a word for emphasis.

Rub-ons

Rub-ons, once used for graphic design, have come back with the popularity of scrapbooking. They give a unique look to a journal page that is different from the effect of a rubber stamp, sticker, or collaged graphic item. Because it has a transparent background, whatever it is placed on will show through. Check out the scrapbook aisles in your local craft stores to find some rub-ons that suit your style. Luckily, old rub-on press type from pre-computer days can still be found on eBay and at garage sales!

[How to Use It]

Lay the rub-on sheet on your journal page, placing the design you want to use where you want it on the page. Be sure the design is facing down with its plastic carrier sheet on top. With one hand securely holding the sheet down, use the supplied burnishing stick to rub over the entire design until it looks frosty. That means it has been transferred to the paper. Carefully pull the carrier sheet back while still holding part of it down, to be sure all of the design is transferred without moving the page. If it's not completely transferred, put it back down and rub over the areas that need to be transferred. If designs other than the one you want are transferring to the journal page, cut out just the one you want.

Glitter Glue

Glitter glue is clear glue with colorful, shiny glitter in it. I'm drawn to it like a moth to a flame. It dries clear, leaving the glitter attached to to whatever it's applied to. It's best applied as a final layer. Squeeze it onto the page where you want it, then spread it out with a paint brush. It comes in every size and color imaginable.

Dymo Label Maker

The handheld gadget that I prefer to use is the Dymo label maker. It embosses letters onto a colored plastic label that is 3/8" (1 cm) wide and it's adhesive, making it perfect for a journal page. They were very popular in the '60s and '70s, and luckily they are still around! To use, simply turn the dial to the first letter of the word, and then squeeze the handle, embossing the letter into the tape. Go to the next letter, press again, and keep going.

COLOR MEDIA

This section of materials is the largest because it covers all the different supplies and many ways to add color to a journal page. Other materials can definitely be used, but these are the ones I use most. Watch the companion DVD to see how I apply these items.

Tools for Applying Paint

Paint can be applied to the page in quite a few ways, including with your fingers, for different looks. As I work, I use many methods at different times, depending on the look I want to achieve. Some of these tools are not only for applying paint but also for removing it.

Fingers

Painting with your fingers is very tactile and gratifying. While working in my journal, I generally use only my fingers to apply or move paint around in small areas. For larger areas, I use one of the other methods because they're faster.

Baby Wipes and Paper Towels

Baby wipes go far beyond their intended use. They really help me get a rich, layered look. You can build up layer after layer of paint, each time scrubbing away areas with the baby wipes to unveil what is underneath. They can remove paint and also move it around. Use the alcohol-free ones because they are gentler on your hands. For me, baby wipes are a must-have, and I thank Juliana Coles for introducing them to me. Buy the inexpensive, generic ones.

Paper towels, being dry, don't remove as much paint and they also won't spread it as far. Either can be an advantage depending whether you want to remove a lot or a little paint.

Credit Cards

Old credit cards are fabulous for quickly spreading paint across a surface. They produce unique, broad, "blobby" shapes of concentrated paint that you can't get with any other method and leave a very thin layer of paint. Although I prefer the plastic cards, I save all the faux cardboard ones I get in the mail for this purpose.

Brushes

Choose the size of the brush based on how detailed the application will be. Cheap 1" (2.5 cm) flat brushes are great for applying gesso, adhesive, and paint. For smaller areas or for applying a paint wash, use a smaller brush you can control better, usually a round one. For stenciling, use a kids' fat paintbrush with stiff bristles. If the bristles are too long, just give them a haircut to make them shorter and stiffer. Be sure to put them into a container with water after using them so that the paint, gesso, or glue doesn't dry and ruin them. Flat sponge brushes can also apply paint, gesso, or adhesive and are inexpensive.

Using a baby wipe to spread paint that was first applied with a credit card

Removing paint with a baby wipe

Spreading paint onto the page with a credit card

Applying acrylic paint with a paint brush

Gesso

Gesso is a thick, paintlike liquid that prepares a surface for painting. It keeps wet media from soaking through the page to the other side and tones down the surface on a page from a printed book. It also helps strengthen thin pages, making it possible to use an old book with delicate pages. Applying gesso can be the very first step in creating a journal page, or some background collaging can be done first and then the gesso applied on top of that.

Gesso, like all of the other art supplies, comes in a wide variety of qualities and textures. I prefer the inexpensive kind over the higher-quality ones. Because I do a lot of writing on my journal pages, it has to be smooth and accepting of pens and markers. You'll have to try out different brands to see what you prefer. Gesso also comes in different colors. For my purposes, I use white or tan since I'm adding color on top of it.

Gesso can be tinted with colored chalk pastels as it's applied to the page. Scribble on the page first with one or more pastel colors, and then apply the gesso on top, smearing the color around.

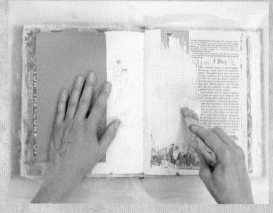

This shows applying gesso with a brush to a printed page. The scribbles are from testing some pens.

Spreading gesso with a baby wipe after it was applied with a brush

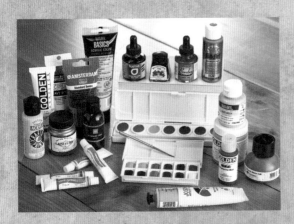

Paints and Inks

Aside from collage, paints and inks are the standard materials for adding a large amount of color to an art journal page.

Acrylic Paint

Acrylic paint can quickly cover a large area with color. Consider using all types of acrylic paint, from inexpensive craft paint to high-end, heavy-body acrylics such as Golden and Liquitex. The higher quality the paint, the more pigment in it, giving bright, vibrant colors. Heavy-bodied acrylic paints are thick but can be watered down and even used for washes, which are more transparent. Golden Fluid Acrylics—liquid but very concentrated paints—are excellent as a wash. Even though they are already liquid, they need to be watered down; otherwise, the piece might be sticky when it dries.

Inexpensive craft paints have less pigment and are already thinner than the heavy-body acrylics, so not as much water needs to be used. Craft paints also come in nice metallic colors that are fun to use.

[How to Use It]

Paint can be applied directly to the page or onto a palette by squirting it on if it comes in a squeeze container or spooning it on if it comes in a jar. Then use a brush, credit card, paper towel, baby wipe, or your fingers to spread the paint around as desired. (See "Tools for Applying Paint," page 21.)

Build layers of colors by adding paint and scrubbing parts of it off, going back and forth. Thin layers make it possible to write on top of the paint after it's dry. Thick layers can become too plasticky and hard to write on. Even with all the paint layers, what is on the background usually shows through, adding visual texture and interest.

To paint a wash, put a small amount of paint on a palette. Get your paint brush fairly wet and touch the side of the paint on your palette. That way you get just a little paint on your brush. Apply as desired. Adding a wash over your work can help tie all the elements together so they don't look disjointed. If the area where you applied the paint wash seems too wet, you can blot it with a paper towel. If this takes too much paint off (because it was mainly water), just reapply more paint.

This detail shows that the texture of the gesso brush marks, the printing on the old book page, and the layers of paint all show through.

 Before adding more paint, make sure it is dry. Otherwise things could tear or the colors could mix together and look like mud.

Using watercolor to fill in outlined letters

Using diluted ink as a color wash over the painted page

Using a thin pickup stick dipped in ink to write

Different kinds of crayon-type tools

Watercolor

Watercolors are transparent paints that come in tubes as a thick liquid with the consistency of toothpaste, in small pans as dried little cakes, or even in color sheets with dried concentrated color on them. (Peerless Watercolor sheets are the only sheets I have found.) The form they come in has nothing to do with the quality. With watercolors from a tube, it's easier to paint larger areas and get more vibrant colors because you can get a higher concentration of paint. On the flip side, the compact size of the pans of watercolors and the ease of the watercolor sheets make them very transportable.

If I write and collage in my journal without painting first, I often add watercolor after I'm done writing. The transparent quality makes it perfect for painting on top of writing, stamping, and doodles as long as everything used before is permanent and waterproof. When I clip a sentence from a book and collage it onto my journal page, I sometimes use watercolor to tint the clipping, toning down the starkness of the white background.

Inks

Different kinds of inks, such as watercolor, acrylic, India, sumi, and calligraphy, can be used to add color to a page or picture or to write with. Some are permanent, some aren't, and they come in all different colors. Depending on the desired effect, inks can be used straight or diluted with water to create a wash or to stain paper with a color. They are fun to use and can be found in the art supply or calligraphy section of hobby and art supply stores.

[How to Use It]

If the bottle has an eyedropper in it, squeeze the end with the dropper in the bottle to get some ink, and then squirt a small amount onto a palette. Dilute the ink if desired with a wet brush or just apply it to the paper. If there isn't a dropper, dip a clean brush into the bottle and first apply it to a palette so that it can be diluted or apply it directly to the paper.

To write with ink, dip a thin stick, such as a pickup stick, skewer, or wooden double-pointed knitting needle, into the bottle, and then write in the journal with it, redipping to get more ink as needed. Thicker inks work best for writing.

Crayon-Type Tools

Crayon-type tools easily add color to a journal page in a more controlled way than paints. The different kinds are all applied in somewhat the same way but have different effects. Generally, I use crayons for finishing touches of color or on borders and use paint for larger areas of color.

Water-Soluble Oil Pastels

These are special creamy crayons that can be blended on paper with your finger. They are best for adding color when you are almost finished with a journal spread because you usually can't write on top of them, except with a paint pen. If they are used early in the process, use them where there won't be writing, like around the borders. They can be found in art supply stores, and some office supply stores carry them in the art supply section. They come in sets of twelve, twenty-four, and forty-eight and really aren't that expensive. I have seen only one brand: Portfolio Series Water-Soluble Oil Pastels.

[How to Use It]

To use water-soluble oil pastels, either dip the tips into water and then color with them or color with them and use a wet paintbrush on top to smear or blend the colors. I skip the water and just use my finger to smear or blend them. How much they blend depends on the paper you are working on. Use these around the edges of photos to help integrate them into the piece.

Watercolor Crayons

Think of watercolor crayons as watercolors trapped in a crayon body. You can draw and scribble with them, but water is needed to set them free and give the watercolor effect. Although they can be used for the same purpose as water-soluble oil pastels, they aren't as soft. When I want a creamy, blended look, I use water-soluble oil pastels. When I want a watercolor-crayon combo look, I use watercolor crayons. As with water-soluble oil pastels, it's hard to write on top of watercolor crayons.

[How to Use It]

Use watercolor crayons like water-soluble oil pastels, but you'll need water to blend them. I like to dip them into water to color with them. They can also be used dry, then brushed over them with a damp brush to blend or give the watercolor effect. Once they are wet on the page, a finger can be used to spread them around.

Crayons

As a kid, I colored outside the lines and didn't care. Using crayons in my work reminds me to work freely like a child, without worrying what others think. I like to use crayons to scribble around and add color at the finishing stages. Since they are waxy, it's hard to write over them. Inexpensive kids' crayons work fine. I recently found metallic crayons . . . YUM!

Smearing the color from a water-soluble oil pastel with my finger

Using a watercolor crayon with the tip first dipped in water

Scribbling with a crayon

TIP When I use crayon-type tools a on a journal spread, I seal the page with a workable fixative to be sure the color doesn't transfer onto the other side of the page when the book is closed.

An assortment of pens, pencils, and markers

Using a pen to outline a stamped image

Pens and Pencils

Pens and pencils are used in art journaling mainly for writing but also for doodling, drawing, or adding color. My favorite ones are brush markers.

Pens

Use pens in your art journal not only for writing, but for their precise lines when doodling or embellishing. There are so many on the market, that it would be impossible to name them. Many of my favorite pens are made by Japanese companies. Pens will work differently on different surfaces. When pen shopping, take along your journal or a loose page painted and collaged so you can try the pens out on the surface most like what they will be used on. Gel pens are wonderful, but some of them skip on painted surfaces. Look for pens that write smoothly without skipping and ones that don't hemorrhage ink on the paper. I prefer permanent or waterproof pens, but when working with ones that aren't, I just remember to use them after I'm done painting. The only way to know if you'll like a pen is to try it out. Buy a single pen to test-drive it. If you like it, buy more in different colors or a set, if they come that way.

Favorite Pens

Some of my favorite pens are the Petit 1 mini fountain pens and the Latte Sweets mini gel pens, both by Pilot. They write on just about any surface, and the mini size is perfect to throw in an art travel bag for journaling away from home. I also really like the gloss of the Glaze gel pens and the opacity of the Soufflé pens, both made by Sakura. They write on most surfaces and dry slightly three-dimensional. Art journalists are always searching for the holy grail of white pens. I recently discovered a good one that doesn't skip: the Hybrid Gel Grip K118 by Pentel. The Glaze white pen is also good. It reminds me of writing with an invisible ink pen when I was a kid, but this one magically turns white as it dries. For continually updated information on favorite pens, go to my website at TraciBunkers.com.

TIP Pens will last longer if they are stored flat instead of upright (except fountain pens, which should be stored upright with the nib pointing up). Sakura, inventor of the gel pen, says their gel pens can be stored in any direction. But when they are dropped into an upright pen container, it's the impact of being dropped over time that is their demise. I say it's better to be safe and store them flat. JetPens, a store that sells a wide selection of Japanese pens, suggests heating the tip of a finicky gel pen with a hair dryer to get it to work again.

Markers

Markers are fun for drawing or writing. You can use all different kinds of markers, ranging from inexpensive kids' markers to high-end art markers. Check out the school supply section and kids' craft section of different stores to see what fun (and inexpensive) ones you can find. Visit the art supply section for some nice ones. And consider using metallic markers, fine markers, and brush markers too. Some of my favorite markers, especially the brush markers, are Japanese.

Much of the information provided for pens holds true for markers. Some are better than others, and page surfaces make a big difference. Some will work just fine, and then when they are used over a certain medium, they stop working, just like that, and can't be revived. I prefer to use permanent markers, but a watercolor effect can be achieved with ones that aren't.

Writing with a marker

Adding color with a watercolor pencil

Going over the watercolor pencil with a damp brush to give a watercolor effect

Favorite Markers

The main markers I use for writing are Faber-Castell PITT pens because they have permanent India ink and come in different nib sizes, including brush. They write on many surfaces and they won't bleed if you add anything on top of them. Sharpie Poster-Paint markers also write on anything and are both vibrant and opaque. I prefer the water-based version, but they also come in oil-based. I love the many colors available in Copic markers. They are refillable and even have interchangeable nibs. Because they are alcohol based, the colors can be blended together. My favorite permanent brush "marker" for writing is the Pentel Pocket Brush Pen. Marketed for Asian calligraphy, the brush tip is an actual bristle brush, which gives great line variation. I have been using one of these for many years, and the brush is still in excellent shape. For more information on my love of pens and markers, go to my website at TraciBunkers.com.

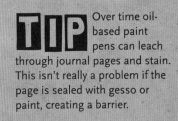

TIP Over time oil-based paint pens can leach through journal pages and stain. This isn't really a problem if the page is sealed with gesso or paint, creating a barrier.

Colored Pencils and Watercolor Pencils

Colored pencils and watercolor pencils can be used for drawing or adding color to your art journal. The benefit of watercolor pencils is that they can be used normally as colored pencils, but added water produces a watercolor effect. These come in all different brands and quality, but the nicer ones are in art supply stores or the art supply section of hobby stores.

Stamping materials

A foam sheet is used as a cushion under the paper while stamping to help stamp a better image.

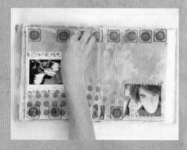

TIP To create a line or border of stamped images equally spaced, stamp the corners or ends first. Then stamp between those two in the middle. Keep stamping in the middle between stamped images until the space between them is too small to stamp.

STAMPS & STAMP PADS

Stamps can be used decoratively, to create borders, to add text, or just for visual impact. I use everything from commercial stamps, stamps that I design and sell, and hand-carved or handmade stamps. It's so much fun to make your own stamps, and it's not that hard. (See my book, *Print & Stamp Lab,* for information on making your own stamps, stencils, and printing tools.)

In hobby stores, rubber stamps are usually sold already mounted. Indie-designed stamps (like mine) often come as an unmounted rubber sheet with several designs or the whole alphabet on it. In that form, they can be cut out and either permanently mounted on wooden blocks or rubber stamp mounting foam or they can be attached to cling cushion for use on clear acrylic blocks. Cling cushion and acrylic blocks make a temporary mounting method that takes up less space, but the stamps have to be properly stored on acetate sheets. I don't want the process for using temporarily mounted stamps slowing me down when I work, so I permanently mount all of my stamps and house them in decorated cigar boxes. It's all a personal preference. Because of their popularity, craft stores now carry a wide variety of clear polymer stamps ready to be used on clear acrylic blocks.

Use permanent ink if you like to do a lot of layering with paint so the ink won't run or bleed—which could be interesting but might not be the desired effect. If you want to use a nonpermanent stamp pad, wait until you've done all the layering with wet media. When using alcohol-based stamp pads, do not leave the top off for very long. The alcohol will evaporate, drying the stamp pad.

Because I mainly use permanent stamp pads, I don't bother cleaning my stamps—the ink is dry on the stamp before I can clean it off. Use alcohol-free baby wipes to wipe nonpermanent ink off stamps.

Press the stamp on the stamp pad and stamp onto the paper. To create a background or a border, repeat the process, stamping a pattern. If the stamped image is too distracting for a background, apply a thin layer of paint over it. Large or detailed stamps with thin lines will print better with a cushion under the page, such as a thin sheet of craft foam, to ensure full contact. Often I like to embellish my stamped images, especially stamped headline text, by outlining the design or letters with pens or markers.

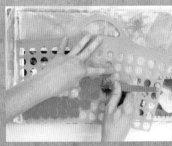

Using part of a plastic basket as a stencil

STENCILS

You can get all kinds of stencils in craft and art supply stores. Look in different departments for different kinds, including the drafting and architectural department. Alphabet stencils are usually in the sign-making section. You can also use scrapbooking die-cut paper made out of thin chipboard as a stencil. Keep an eye out for things you already have to use as "found" stencils, such as doilies and game pieces.

[How to Use It]

Place the stencil down on the page. Dab a stencil brush or chunky kids' paintbrush in paint. Holding the edges of the stencil with one hand and the brush straight up with the other hand, tap the brush on top of the stencil to push the paint through the open areas. Move the brush around, adding more paint to it as needed, until the desired area is stenciled.

You can use a brush and paint for stenciling, but a small raised stamp pad can be used in the same way. You can also use stencils as templates and trace around or scribble inside the cut-out area with pens, pencils, or markers. You'll need to experiment to see what materials work best for the stencil you are using to get the desired results.

COLLAGE MATERIALS & IMAGERY

Collage material can come from many sources, such as wrapping paper, maps, candy wrappers, magazine clippings, and your own photographs. Anything is fair game to glue into your journal.

Although you can use found photos from magazines, use your own photographs to make your work more personal. Even if you aren't a photographer and have only an inexpensive point-and-shoot camera, start taking pictures to use in your journal. Once you get into the habit and have a nice supply of photos, you'll feel more connected to the journal pages where you use them.

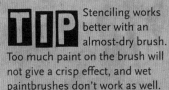

TIP Stenciling works better with an almost-dry brush. Too much paint on the brush will not give a crisp effect, and wet paintbrushes don't work as well.

This shows using tape to hinge a religious card. The tape is applied from the reverse side of the page and folded over to the back of the card.

Using another piece of tape to finish hinging the religious card on the front

Before attaching the paper, it is folded where it will fit into the center of the book.

Collaging the paper onto the book, working it into the crease

Ephemera

Ephemera is basically a fancy word for different things made out of paper. The great advantage is that such items are free and just about anything can be used for collage material. Over time, you will get a feel for what you like to use and begin to edit your collections. You can also swap your scraps with art friends.

Joss paper is a favorite of many book artists. It's colorful or decorated paper that traditionally is burned during ceremonies and holidays in Eastern cultures. It's usually sold in packets and comes in many styles. In international districts in large cities, often there are stores that sell only Joss paper. You can also find it in some Asian grocery stores.

Ephemera can be collaged down on a journal page to become part of the background, or it can be glued down later as an integral piece. Either way, it adds visual interest, even if it's just barely peeking through some thin layers of paint. Don't be afraid to cover ephemera up, even partially. Sometimes what I have collaged down isn't even visible by the time I finish, but it was a stepping-stone, leading me to the finished page.

[How to Use It]

If necessary, tear or cut the ephemera to the desired shape and size. Decide how you want to attach it, whether with staples, brads, sewing, or adhesive, and attach it to the page. Be sure it is attached well, especially if paint will be applied on top of it. If the edges start to come up, it can be fixed with tape, staples, or more collage material.

If you want both sides of something to show, either attach a clear envelope to the page and put the piece in it or hinge the piece to the edge of the page or anywhere on the spread. Use tape to create a hinge on the piece of ephemera or on the envelope. It could also be attached as a hanging piece. Punch a hole in it, thread some yarn or thread through the hole, knot the ends, and staple or tape it to the page near the knot.

Photographs

Creating Your Own Imagery

Using your own photos in your journal pages makes the pages more personal. You don't have to fancy yourself a photographer to take pictures for your journal. You also don't need expensive equipment. I love low-fi photography, where the photos are created with low-tech equipment, such as the plastic point-and-shoot cameras that use film. I use the actual prints right in my journal. (See the "Call to Action: Photo Field Trip" on page 88, which uses low-fi cameras.) I also enjoy snapping a picture with my cell phone and printing it from my computer.

As I'm working in my journal, I don't want to have to stop to get anything, especially to print a picture. For that reason, after I take pictures I deal with them soon after. If they are digital, I print them out in different sizes, ganging up several pictures on the same page. If they are print film, I take the film to get developed as soon as I finish the roll. Then I put them in my stash folders with other photos and ephemera, ready to use. This works well with my journaling style since I don't worry about trying to find the right subject matter with my images. I just grab what I'm drawn to at the time.

Chances are you already have a camera of some sort, so use it! Start carrying it with you and finding beauty in everyday objects and surroundings. Photograph them to make the ordinary extraordinary.

Digital Cameras

Digital cameras make it really easy to take your own pictures, and you don't need an expensive or fancy one. My favorite is a kids' low-resolution digital camera. The pictures look very funky and artsy because their resolution is so low. I also enjoy using my "real" digital camera because I can get super detail on objects, zooming in much closer than I can with my eyes alone. This can create interesting abstract photos that make good background images. If you don't have a digital camera but are interested in buying one, used ones are often available on eBay at a good price. Before buying anything, think about what you want in a camera to help narrow your decision. Also check camera reviews online and ask friends for recommendations. A little bit of research can help a lot.

TIP The most common mistake in photography is to shoot from too far away. The photo has no central focus—nothing to draw you in. Get closer, take close-up shots, or zoom right in. You'll get more interesting results. Before you push the button, look at the whole image to see exactly what will be in the shot. In art school, my photo teacher taught me a valuable lesson. Crop with the camera! Do all the work as you're taking the picture so you don't have to mess with them on the computer.

Webcams

Webcams might seem like an odd choice for taking pictures, but they can be a lot of fun. Most of them are only for PCs, but some work on Macintoshes as well. Luckily for Macintosh users, a driver called macam helps Macs use cameras and webcams that normally work only on PCs. It can be downloaded at http://webcam-osx.sourceforge.net. Before downloading it, check the list of cameras and webcams to see which ones will work on the Macintosh.

Although webcams are stationary, limiting what can be photographed, just get creative! They are great for self-portraits, and objects can be held up in front of the camera. I have done different series where I have held my pets or dolls and taken our pictures, It's fast, and you can see right away if you like the results or need to reshoot. Depending on the resolution of the webcam, it could be crystal clear, or you could get funky, low-res, artsy-looking pictures (which I'm all about!). After taking the pictures, print them out for your art journal.

Many computers now have built-in webcams. Macintosh users with a built-in camera have a program called Photo Booth, which makes it super simple to take pictures, and special effects can even be selected before taking the picture. I use this frequently, especially for quick self-portraits. If you don't have Photo Booth, try the online "photo booth" at http://picturenest.net. As long as you have a webcam, you can take four pictures hooked in a strip, just like the old-time photo booths. From the site, the picture strip can be sent via email or shared on social networking sites such as Facebook. It can also be saved in your computer to print out and use in your artwork.

Camera Phones

Many cell phones can now take pictures. The pictures are small, and depending on the phone, the resolution isn't necessarily great, but most have adjustable settings for better pictures. Also, the phone is small and usually with you, so it's easy to take a picture whenever you want, wherever you are. My camera phone is very inexpensive but does a pretty good job of taking pictures as long as there is enough light.

Pictures from camera phones can be printed from a computer, a photo lab, or a Polaroid PoGo instant printer. Check the manual to see how to best do it with your setup. Some phones can print wirelessly to a printer. I send the picture as a message to my email address to get it on my computer. Then I print it either from my printer or via Bluetooth to my PoGo printer. Sometimes I take it into a photo editing program and tweak it a little or enlarge it before printing.

Instant Cameras and Printers

Polaroid, well known for instant cameras, stopped producing their instant film and cameras around 2008 and made many artists and photographers, including myself, very sad. But their PoGo instant mobile printer and PoGo instant camera are still around. They print 3" x 2" (7.6 x 5.1 cm) adhesive-backed photos, about the size of a business card. The printer is small and portable and the prints are on adhesive paper, perfect for an art journal. A Bluetooth-enabled computer or camera phone can print to it wirelessly, or a PictBridge-enabled camera can print to it by connecting a USB cable. The camera version is basically the PoGo printer with a camera all in one. The printer and camera print on special-color thermal paper, so no ink cartridge or toner is needed. My cell phone won't work with the PoGo printer, so I send the pictures to my computer and from there send them to the printer. My digital camera hooks up directly to the PoGo printer with a USB cable.

This shows peling the adhesive backing from a PoGo print to attach to the journal page. The picture was taken with a camera phone.

Old Polaroid film is still available through eBay and other sites, but it has become extremely expensive. Luckily a group called the Impossible Project (www.the-impossible-project.com) took over production of Polaroid film, so many kinds are available again but are still more expensive than they were originally. When Polaroid stopped making instant film and cameras, Fujifilm started making them. The films are a different size, so most won't fit into the old Polaroid cameras, but some of the peel-apart kind will. Fujifilm makes two kinds of instant cameras, called Instax. The regular Instax, which is what I have, produces photos that look like Polaroids, with a shiny surface and an image area of about 4" x 2 1/2" (10.2 x 6.4 cm). The Instax Mini prints Polaroid-type photos about the size of a business card.

Any of these instant cameras and printers is perfect for art journaling. I'm all about instant gratification, so it's fun to run out and snap a few photos to either use right then in my art journal or to save for later. PoGo prints can be attached by simply peeling the backing off and sticking the picture into the journal. Other instant photos can be attached with adhesive, staples, brads, or tape (see "Adhesives," page 16, and "Attachment Tools," page 18). Of course, copies can be made of the instant pictures, but I just go for it and use the original.

Film Cameras

Even though film cameras sadly seem to be going the way of dinosaurs, I wanted to include them. I can be all fancy with my digital toys, but I'm "old school" at heart and love to shoot film cameras. I love to use the very basic, plastic ones often referred to as toy cameras and attach the actual photos from the photo lab into my journal. Karen Michel, who is also old school, taught me different ways to alter real photos, making them a lovely addition to an art journal. Read all about it in her book, *The Complete Guide to Altered Imagery*. If you don't have a film camera but want to give it a try, check out your local thrift stores or hit garage sales. I've even found cameras at the dollar store! They often have light leaks, creating red streaks across the picture, or produce funky, blurry images, which make them all the better in my eyes! Often you can find outdated film at a discount, which is still fine to use and sometimes adds to the funky quality.

Magazine Imagery and Words

As much as I love taking my own pictures for my art journal, flipping through a magazine to cut out pictures, words, and sentences is gratifying and soothing. I look at magazines in a different way when I'm doing this. I don't look for anything in particular, just images and words that catch my eye. Even in advertisements, parts of phrases in large or small type can be perfect for a yet-to-be-created journal page. I cut them out, keep the smaller pieces in a glassine envelope so I don't lose them, and put the larger images in my stash folders.

Magazines are great for journaling imagery because they have a broad range of photos of places, people, and situations that we might never have the chance to photograph ourselves. Personalize the image by making it part of the journal page—not just an image on it—when you paint, stamp, and draw on it.

WORKING DETAILS

CHAPTER 3:

hile trying to work in your art journal, you could encounter some stumbling blocks. The concepts in this chapter will help the creating and journaling process flow more freely. You will learn ways to get unstuck, how to tie elements together, and how to add text to your pages. Please read this information before diving into the journaling exercises. It might save you from frustration later.

GETTING UNSTUCK

Traci says, "Don't know what to do? Are you drawing a blank? Then you're thinking too much. Get your hands moving and just be in the moment and what you need to do will come to you."

You may feel stuck at times or at a loss for what to do. It could mean you're thinking too much or trying to force something. In this case, the best thing to do is to just start working, no matter what that work is. Using your hands engages the other side of your brain and helps stop the monkey mind. It's a way to distract yourself productively to break through to what needs to come out.

If you are stuck before even starting on a journal page, it's simple. Begin by applying a layer of gesso or collage some papers down. Slap on some paint. Don't worry about what it's going to end up being about because it doesn't matter. It's all an evolution. The way it starts will be very different from the way it ends; it's all good. Then start adding some images you like. Before you know it, you're writing on the page too. If you're still stuck and didn't get to any writing, prepare and paint some more pages. Then they'll be ready for when you get to them, things are flowing, and you want to get started right away!

I find usually when people are blocked while working on a journal page, they are working teeny-tiny, writing teeny-tiny, or drawing teeny-tiny and trying to control things. This gets them closed into a tighter space and frame of mind, basically blocking themselves in. In this situation, try a different tool, a bigger marker, or bigger paintbrush, one that you have less control over. This is something I remember from drawing classes in art school. If my drawing started to get too rigid, the teacher would have me use a fat piece of graphite or large oil pastel instead of a precise little controlled pencil. The lack of control gives you no choice but to let go and loosen up, unclogging the tightness, allowing things to flow more freely.

Another thing I like to do when I'm stuck is to flip through a magazine or two, not spending more than five or ten minutes, cutting out pictures and words. Then pick out one of the pictures or phrases, glue it down, and go from there.

Better yet, when you're feeling stuck, ask yourself what's going on. What's the problem? What are you avoiding or afraid to journal about? This is a great time to do the journaling exercise "Checking In," on page 100.

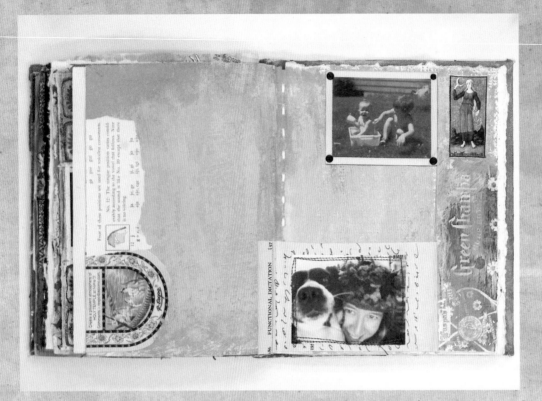

Different items on a journal page, looking disjointed

Applying a light wash of acrylic paint over certain areas to unify the elements.

TYING THE ELEMENTS TOGETHER

It is pretty normal for the elements and items on a journal page to look disjointed, like they don't belong together, or like they were just plopped down on the page, not really fitting in. Some simple solutions will tie everything together.

The quickest and easiest fix is to do a light color wash over the whole page or the items that seem to stick out because they are white or brighter. (See "Paints and Inks," page 23.) If washing over only certain items, use a color that matches the other items. The light color wash helps tie the pieces together, unifying them by color. It also tones down the stark background from words clipped out of books and magazines.

Photographs or images can be tied into the journal spread in other ways. Applying something that crosses from the background onto the photo or image will help ground it, whether it's paint, tape, sewing, collage, drawing, or even writing. Crossing over boundaries to bring things together pertains to any collaged items. Water-soluble oil pastels or watercolor crayons can be used along the edges of an item, blended out, to help soften the edges and meld them into the background. Cutting out the subject's silhouette will also eliminate that hard edge. Basically anything that will break up or soften the hard edge of a photo, image, or collaged piece will help tie it to the journal page.

Continuing the writing over parts of the photograph helps tie it together with the whole page.

Stitching the photo and blending the other edges with water-soluble oil pastels breaks up the photo's hard edges, melding it with the other elements.

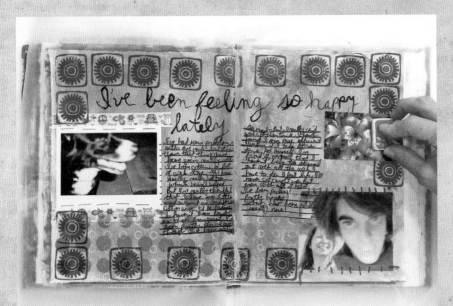

Continuing the stamped border on top of a photo helps to join it with the journal page. Tape on the top and bottom of the photo on the left helps in the same way.

ADDING TEXT OR WRITING

A finished journal page showing different methods of adding text

A page with writing in an attached envelope

Deciding which computer-generated text to use

Depending on how you're feeling, you may want to start writing or adding text early, or you might do just about everything before adding the words. You could end up with a lot of space for the writing or with not much. Work with what you have—there are many ways to add the text or words.

I unconsciously always have a headline of sorts on my journal pages and then write by hand what I want to express. It's just what I always seem to do, and it works for me. I usually create the headline either by stamping with alphabet rubber stamps or by drawing outline letters and filling them in with markers or colored pencils. I also like to write the headline with a stick dipped in ink. All of these make a bold statement.

If the background or area where you want to write or stamp words is too dark, use a white pen or white stamp pad or lighten the area with white paint or a lighter color of paint. Gesso can also be used to lighten an area.

If there just isn't room for the writing and you don't want to cover anything up to add it, write on a separate piece of paper. The paper can then be attached at the edge of a page as a foldout, or it can be folded up and put into some kind of envelope attached to the spread. Writing that is on paper inside an envelope lets you express yourself without being visible on the page. The act of expression still happens, but the outcome is protected.

When you're ready to do the main writing, you can just use a pen or marker or draw or stamp lines first as writing guides. Besides acting as a guide, the lines add to the overall look of the journal page. I use a pen, pencil, or marker to quickly draw the lines, or I use a rubber stamp of hand-drawn lines that I designed. If I feel my writing doesn't show up as much as I'd like it to, I just go back over it with the same writing tool or use a different color to help it show up more.

You might add more text with smaller alphabet stamps or a Dymo Label Maker or you could print text from a computer, cut it out, and paste it down. I like to handwrite the main part of my message because I feel more connected to it that way. I usually print out only a phrase or two from my computer to add in this fashion. When I use the computer to generate text, I print it in a few different fonts, sizes, and colors so I can pick which one works best with the journal page. To create reverse text, make the text box black or a desired color, and then make the text white or another color. I like to cut it out in strips and attach it with a glue stick.

I also like to cut out random sentences from old books and save them in glassine envelopes. When I want to use one of them, I glue it to the journal page. This is also how I use phrases, words, and sentences I've cut out of magazines.

Affixing the text with a glue stick after cutting it into strips

LETTING GO

When teaching workshops, I've noticed that many times people bring too much "stuff" to use. Because of that, they spend more time digging through their supplies to find the right picture or the perfect stamp than they do working on the exercise. Maybe this is a way to actually avoid working? I find that sometimes limiting yourself in the supplies that you use will help you to be more creative. Instead of trying to find that perfect picture, just use the one you like. If something is too big, instead of searching for something else, just cut it smaller. A part of all of this is to let go and not be as concerned with the final outcome.

I don't agonize over what items to collage down or what pictures to use when I'm working. I just grab what I'm drawn to or what's within reach, and glue it down. Often the imagery I use in my journal pages seems to have nothing in common with other elements or with what I'm journaling about. I just use it because I like it. In the end, it all comes together and works as a whole. Frequently things that I was drawn to, but that seemed to have no meaning, become very important in helping me reach that "aha!" moment. I make connections or have realizations I wouldn't have had if I had been more controlling of the images or supplies I used. Not laboring over these things helps me to work more intuitively and makes my work richer in meaning and uncontrived. I work without any preconceived idea of what my journal page will look like. The finished page isn't what's important. The process, or even the act of just doing, is.

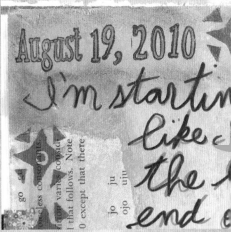

Two different ways to date a journal page

DATING YOUR PAGES

This is the last thing you need to know before starting. I feel it's very important to date your journal pages, whether you write the date on or stamp it with a date stamp. An art journal documents your life and journey through self-realization and growth. Dating everything helps you later remember that period or issue and helps put a time frame on everything. It has helped me to realize how long I was dealing with a specific issue or to notice cycles of dealing with physical pain, depression, or other concerns. In creating the journal pages for this book, I didn't date any of them so that they wouldn't be tied to a specific time or seem outdated. But I normally always date my pages.

CHAPTER 4:

This chapter is what you've been waiting for. It's the meat and potatoes of this book. The mixed-media materials and foundation information have been covered, and now it's time to put it all together and get to the real work.

There are three sections of exercises in this chapter: "Journaling Prompts and Exercises," "Call to Action Exercises," and "Self-Care Exercises." While these sections overlap, each inviting introspection and journaling, they are all slightly different. All of the exercises will be like taking a journaling workshop with me, except that I won't be there to push you along. You'll need to do that yourself. They all also use mixed-media materials to convey personal expression either in a visual journal spread in your book or with a project outside of the book.

Be sure you read the information about the various mixed-media materials and chapter 3 before you begin any exercises, but if a question comes up while you are working on an exercise, refer back to previous sections as needed. Don't let yourself get stuck and ruin the flow of working. The flow is very important, and interruptions can stifle the process. If you can work in your journal only for short periods of time, have everything ready so that when you do have that break, you are all set and can jump right in. Working for short periods on a regular basis is much better than working for just an hour once every few months.

I generally start from a clean journal spread and work on it until I feel I'm finished journaling on that specific theme or issue. You might find a way that works better for you, particularly if you have only short amounts of time to journal. For example, you might want to schedule twenty or thirty minutes a day and make it part of your routine. If time is limited, you can prepare some of the pages in advance by applying a thin layer of gesso or covering them with masking tape or collage and then adding a base layer of paint or washes. When you have time to work, you already have background in place. You can start right in with the inner work and journaling exercises, adding images, paint, and writing to personalize the spread based on the specific feeling you want to express.

When I've finished a journal spread, usually in one or two sittings, I'm done and move on to the next one. Some people like to go back and keep working a page, changing what it's about and letting it evolve. Do whatever works best for you. Find your own rhythm and style. Though you'll see my work in progress in the following exercises, it's simply to give you an idea of how the journaling process works and to inspire you to find your own voice and working style. In this field, I've seen many people who seem to just copy the style of other artists. While this can be expected when starting out, when you are trying out different things and cutting your visual journaling teeth, you will rob yourself of your own personal expression if you don't eventually find your own way of working. Remember, it's not about trying to make a pretty picture; it's about the journey and personal self-discovery.

Note: The exercises can be worked in any order and from any section you choose. But if you are brand new to art journaling, you might want to start with "Getting Started and Digging Deeper" on page 44. Please read completely through the exercise you are working on before starting. That will help you to understand what you will be doing and allow you to gather in advance any specific materials you might want to use.

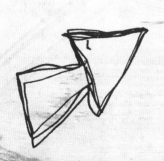  

1.

Taping pages together
with masking tape

CREATING A
THREE-PAGE SPREAD

s you journal, you might decide you need more room to fully
express yourself on a particular spread. It's very easy to attach
another page that folds out to create a three-page spread.
You can do this after you have already started working or
before you start. Choose the page you want to attach and cut or tear it
to the desired height and width if necessary. Be sure it's not too wide to
fit within the book when it's closed. Place the page next to the one you
are attaching it to with the edges flush and tape them together on the
front with masking tape. (Any tape can be used, but masking tape can
be painted to become part of the background.) Tape the whole length of
the pages, whether it's with one long strip or several pieces. If you have
trouble keeping the pages in place while taping, use one or two small
pieces of tape to hold them together. After taping the front, turn and tape
across the join on the back of the pages, leaving a small piece of tape
extending beyond the top and bottom. Fold those pieces over to the front
and tape down.

2.

After taping the other side, the ends of the tape are folded over to the front.

3.

The completed attached page

Lincoln's First Inaugural Address

He started, but the school soon closed. Two years later he went for a few weeks to another school. It was a "blab" school. The pupils all studied their lessons out loud so that the teacher would know they were working. Abraham had only about a year's schooling, but he learned to read and write and to do some arithmetic.

Abraham grew tall and strong. He could handle an ax well and was an expert rail splitter. But he liked to read far better than he liked to plow or split rails. He carried a book to the fields and often stopped to read a little "to catch his breath."

The Ohio River was not many miles from the Lincoln home. When he was 19 Abraham had a chance to go on a flatboat to New Orleans. He had his first glimpse of a city.

In 1830 the Lincoln family moved to Illinois. They settled on the north bank of the Sangamon River. In his first summer in Illinois, Abe, as he was now called, split more than 4,000 rails for fences. After only a little more than a year here, the family moved to another part of Illinois. But Abe did not go with them. He decided to strike out on his own.

Soon Denton Offcutt, a trader, asked Abe to help take a boatload of corn and pork to New Orleans. Lincoln again saw that city. He saw, among other things, the slave market. When he came back from the trip, Offcutt hired him to work as a clerk in his store at New Salem, Ill.

Lincoln reached New Salem on election day. The schoolteacher, Mentor Graham, was writing down the votes. He looked up and saw the tall young stranger. "Can you write?" he asked. Lincoln said he could. Mentor Graham then asked him to help with the election. The two men soon became good friends. Graham's help made up for the schooling Lincoln had missed.

Lincoln was soon well liked in New Salem. He could tell stories well, he could wrestle, and he was so honest he was called "Honest Abe." When fighting broke out with the Indians, Lincoln went to help. He did not get into any actual fighting, but he learned a little about what war meant.

When it was time to elect someone to the state legislature, Lincoln's friends in New Salem persuaded him to run for the office. But he was defeated.

Now Lincoln decided that he would be a lawyer. Offcutt had given up his store, and Lincoln and William T. Berry had started a store of their own. Business was slow. Lincoln had time to read and study law books.

He ran again for the state legislature and was elected. He was re-elected three times. He made many trips between the capital of Illinois and New Salem. After his years in the legislature, he moved to Springfield to practice law.

Lincoln was tall and homely and still poor. But Mary Todd, who had always ha

Visiting the War Wounded

NEW YORK PUBLIC LIBRARY

Powhatan appears in John Smith's 1631 edition of the Generall Historie of Virginia.

The London Company got a head start on the Plymouth Company and in 1607 established what would be the first permanent English town in the present United States. It was named Jamestown, in honor of the king, and American real estate got off to a fast start as John Smith avowed that "heaven and earth never agreed better to frame a place for man's habitation." The original 105 settlers would soon question this extravagant claim, but for the present they could do little but assault the many problems that faced them in the American wilderness.

Complexities of rooting a civilization on a virgin land soon became apparent. Along with the to-be-expected

74

pioneer hardships, the Jamestown settler had to learn to live with the Indian. Powhatan, the powerful chief of the Algonquians, earnestly worked for peace with the Englishman, but Jamestown did suffer sneak attacks by one or another of the villages in Powhatan's confederacy. Yet, despite these sporadic uprisings (sometimes incited by the Spanish to the south), peaceful coexistence was the rule during the difficult early years of the Virginia colony.

As if the external troubles were not enough, however, the men of Jamestown had their own quarrels. The seven-man local council included such strong personalities as Edward-Maria Wingfield and John Smith, and their violent quarrels resulted in division and suffering for all residents. Even more threatening to the little settlement was the incidence of disease. So prevalent was sickness that despite the arrival of two additional groups of people in 1608, the population declined. When in January, 1608, a fire destroyed most of Jamestown's buildings and shortly thereafter rats devoured much of the remaining corn supply, the probability of a permanent settlement in America took a turn for the worse.

The "gentlemen" go on strike

Moreover, there were times when the settlers seemed to be working against their own interests. Some of them took the position that as "gentlemen" they should not work with the

JOURNALING PROMPTS & EXERCISES

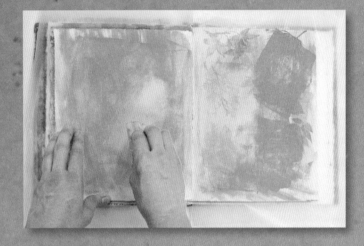

In this section, various exercises and prompts include creating and combining collages, images, and writing for self-introspection. It might be helpful to do these exercises several times, allowing some time to lapse in between, with each session pushing you farther into self-discovery. I can do the same exercise in my journal multiple times and come up with totally different results and insights, depending on what I'm going through at the time and what my struggles or joys are.

PROMPT: GETTING STARTED & DIGGING DEEPER

This exercise is geared toward the beginner but can be helpful to people at any experience level. When I'm teaching journaling workshops, I frequently see students wanting to express themselves on their journal pages but getting stuck early in the process. They stamp or write several vague words and don't know what to do after that. This exercise will help you push through that initial barrier.

Open your journal to an empty spread. Apply a thin layer of gesso to prepare the page so it can be painted without the paint soaking through. Then, covering the whole spread, apply some paint using one or more colors you like. You can apply several thin layers, scrubbing some of the paint off or moving it around with a paper towel or baby wipe before it dries. Then, stamp or write *Dream*, *Imagine*, and *Create*. Feel free to substitute other words that might have more meaning to you. Now work on the page, adding images, stamps, or whatever you like. As you do that, think about what these words mean to you. Ask yourself questions about the words if you need to, even something as simple as "Dream what?" "Create what?" and "Imagine what?" Basically, you are pushing yourself to go beyond just putting a few words on a page and digging deeper to find out what thoughts they trigger. Write about what your dreams are, what you imagine, and what you want to create. This exercise can be done with any words that come to mind, even if you aren't sure why you chose them. Asking simple questions can bring some insight. Keep working on the page, doing more writing or embellishing with markers or tape or ephemera. Work until the page is filled and you feel you are finished. You might find that as you wrote and worked on the pages, more ideas and realizations bubbled up. Turn to another spread and continue working, pushing the ideas to see where they take you. If you get stuck, just start asking yourself more questions.

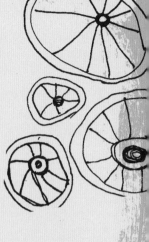

1.
The journal spread before starting

2.

A thin layer of gesso is applied to the pages

3.

Pink, orange, and yellow paint are applied in thin layers and scrubbed off in some areas, creating textures and letting previous layers show through.

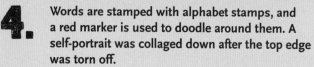

4. Words are stamped with alphabet stamps, and a red marker is used to doodle around them. A self-portrait was collaged down after the top edge was torn off.

5. Decorative tape is added to the sides of the photo to help hold the edges down. The photo is altered with markers. Stamps are stamped around the edges of the paper to create a border.

6. Text is added with markers during the process of questioning what thoughts or feelings the words evoked.

7. A pinhole photograph and a heart-shaped cutout of Joss paper were collaged down. More writing is added.

 Before reusing waxed paper, be sure there isn't any wet paint or adhesive on it that might transfer to another surface. If there is, fold it over to cover the wet glue or paint.

8. The outlined letters are filled in with markers and the stamped letters are outlined with a metallic marker. The radiating lines on the self-portrait are drawn over with a paint marker.

9. Rub-ons and more stamps are added.

10.

Text is stamped with alphabet stamps along the top, and several colors of water-soluble oil pastels and crayons are used to add more colors and scribbles. Circles are drawn with a marker inside the doodles around the main words.

PROMPT:
GRATITUDE

You can't bring more good things into your life until you acknowledge and are thankful for the good things you already have. No matter how hard you think your life is or what kind of problems you are having, there is always something to be grateful for. And recognizing those things will open doors to new possibilities.

This exercise is great to do on a regular basis. If you are in a funk, this will help you get out of it or at least shift your mood. It's also a good warm-up if you feel like working in your journal but don't really know what to do. It gets your hands moving and the juices flowing, and you feel inspired afterward.

To get yourself started, open your journal and prepare a spread however you like, with gesso, paint, and maybe some collage for the background. This is setting the foundation of gratitude, so use colors and items that make you happy. If you feel a little stuck, start by making a list, directly on the spread, of things you are grateful for. Or just jump right in and start adding pictures, drawings, and whatever else might convey your gratitude for these things. Don't forget to write about them as well to fully express your thankfulness. Keep going, adding embellishments, stamps, or more color until the page is filled with colorful joy!

TIP If the baby wipe is too wet and removes too much paint, set a few out to dry a little before using. Also, some kinds of baby wipes hold up well enough to be used as collage material after drying.

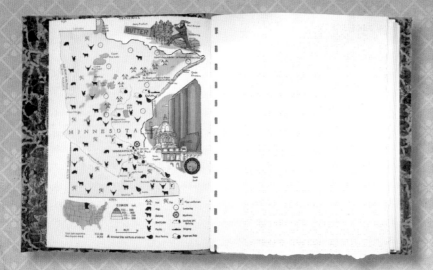

1.

The journal spread before starting

2.

The spread is covered with a light layer of gesso, and then yellow paint is applied with a credit card.

3.

More paint is added in thin layers, covering the whole page.

4. Personal photographs are collaged to the page, and then a tape border is placed around the central self-portrait to help hold the edges down. Words are added with markers and alphabet stamps.

5. Writing is done about the things I'm grateful for. Ruby is stamped onto our picture, and *My fabulous life* is written over with another pen to make it stand out more.

TIP Since I like to take pictures, I frequently shoot things that make me happy. Then I have images ready to go for when I'm working on a gratitude page. If you aren't into photography, you can keep a folder of magazine clippings of things that make you happy.

6. More writing and collage are added, and the outlined letters are colored in with markers.

7. A thin layer of paint is washed over the newly collaged items to tie them in with the other items. Hand-carved stamps are then stamped onto the page.

8. Decorative tape is added and then painted on. A handmade oval stamp is stamped in offset layers of several colors, and some of the previous stampings are outlined with a marker. *My heart is full!* is written near the top with a brush marker.

9. A red water-soluble oil pastel is used to create a border around the photos on the left side, smeared into the background to make the photos meld with the page.

10. *Gratitude* and *Spring* are outlined again so they are more prominent. The strip of photo-booth pictures is embellished with a paint marker, and then various colors are added onto the spread with crayons and water-soluble oil pastels.

PROMPT:
PURGING

Are you holding on to something negative that's holding you back? Someone you're angry with or something you did that you regret? It's time to let it go and move on. Turn to a full spread in your journal where you can write. If you don't have one, make one by covering the pages of a spread with gesso or masking tape. Work quickly so you can get on to the real work.

Take a pen, marker, or something you can write with quickly—something easy to use. No one else will ever read this, so it's safe to let it all out and be done with it. It's time to be honest with yourself about this matter. Write as much as you need to write, as fast as you need to write. Don't censor yourself or worry about how terrible, how petty, or how "whatever" it is. Just do it and purge yourself. Don't stop and think about what to write, just keep writing. Sometimes thinking slows us down and gives the censor time to take over. Leave the censor behind.

If you are stuck, you are thinking too much. Just start writing about what you are feeling or what's bothering you and keep writing until you have nothing more to say on the subject. If it helps, write as if you are writing a letter to yourself or to whomever you are thinking about. Don't stop to find the right words. Keep your hand moving. Usually once you get started, it flows. Attach another sheet of paper if you need to write more (see page 42, "Creating a Three-Page Spread"). Don't read back over what you have already written while you are writing. It's okay if you repeat yourself or ramble. Don't worry about spelling, grammar, or punctuation. It doesn't matter. You just need to get it out. Use a permanent pen or marker so that if you paint on top of it, the ink won't bleed and muddy up the paint.

Turn It Around

You just did the writing, and you got it out. Now it's time to turn it around and do the visual part. Using any desired materials, such as paint, collage, stamps, and markers, create a positive journal spread on top of the writing. Make it about how you want this situation to be now that you have purged and are past it. You can completely obliterate the writing you first did, but it's okay if you just work on top of it, leaving parts of the text peeking through. You won't be able to read the whole thing, so it's safe. Dip into your stash of collage clippings if something there will work for this exercise. As you work, visualize the peaceful, happy resolution and how you feel now that you have moved on. Let this journal spread become your visual affirmation for how things will be. Make it positive because you've let go of the negative.

Remember, the images you use don't have to be a literal representation of what your journal spread is about. They can be things that evoke the feeling you want or have or even just things you like. You can also help express this idea through colors and words. Don't you feel lighter? Now you can move on.

1.

The journal spread before starting

2.

The spread is covered with a light layer of gesso, and then a marker is used to write for the purging process.

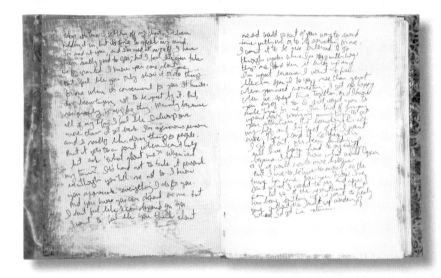

3.

Layers of green, pink, and red paint are applied over the writing.

4. A self-portrait, part of an old book page, and other items are collaged down.

5. A wash of yellow paint is applied on top of the collaged elements to help tie them together.

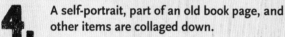

6. Text is added around the self-portrait with alphabet stamps and magazine clippings.

7. More magazine text, a pinhole photograph, a flower border from cardboard packaging, and vintage ephemera are added.

TIP Sometimes this type of purging creates a shift and starts putting things in motion—buried things that you weren't aware of or that you were denying start to surface, causing more awareness and also a need for more purging! Do this exercise whenever you need to, as often as you need to.

8. A brush marker and fine marker are used to add writing.

9. More writing is done with a red marker, and then part of it is written over with black to make it more prominent. Another piece of the flower border is collaged down. Stamps, a rub-on, and a sticker are also added. After *Handle with Care* is stamped, the letters are outlined so they stand out.

10.

A cut-out image of Lakshmi is collaged down. A rub-on and gold sticker stars are also added. The outlined letters of *Win-Win* are filled in with a red marker.

PROMPT:
GET OUT OF YOUR OWN WAY

We always have the answers within us (even if we aren't always aware of them). It's a matter of getting out of our own way and listening or paying attention. Sometimes when I'm stuck, I have a conversation with myself as if I'm talking to my therapist, a mentor, or someone I look up to. I ask whatever I want to know, and then without thinking—or getting in my own way—I answer myself as they would answer. We always think someone else has the answers for us, but this exercise is a way to trick ourselves into tapping into what we already know.

In your journal or on another piece of paper, write down what you need or want to know, what's getting in your way or keeping you from accomplishing something, or what steps you should take to move toward your desired life. Then without thinking, answer yourself as another person would respond. Just start writing whatever comes to mind without censoring yourself. Keep writing, asking, and answering, exploring every aspect, until you've gotten it all out. Now create a spread based on your answer, combining collage with written words, paint, and stamps. If you did the writing in your journal, either work directly on top of the writing as I have or turn to a new spread if you want to be able to later read what you have written. If the writing was done on a separate piece of paper, it can be put into an envelope and attached to the journal spread. (See page 30 for more on hinging a piece of ephemera to the edge of a page.)

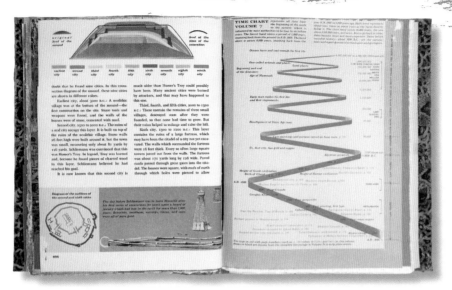

1.

The journal spread before starting

2.

After a light layer of gesso is applied to the spread, the writing is done directly on the page.

3.

Green paint is spread on top of the writing with a baby wipe.

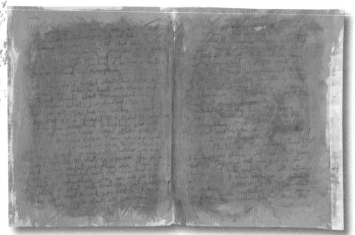

4. Orange paint is applied with a credit card and scrubbed off in areas. Then magenta paint is applied with a brush and moved around with a paper towel, baby wipe, and fingers.

5. Items are collaged down, then painted with a yellow wash. Magenta paint is added to the edges of the collaged hand, blending the edges of the paper into the background. Words are added with alphabet stamps.

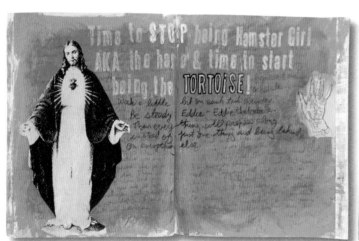

6. The word *Stop* is enhanced with a white pen. *Tortoise* is outlined for emphasis, and writing is added with a marker.

7. A thought balloon saying *Be the Tortoise* is written. A cut-out Image of a tortoise is collaged down, then outlined with a white pen so it stands out. Cut-outs of other deities are added.

TIP Often paint builds up on the underside of the credit card, away from the edge, as it's being used. Change the angle of the card, holding it closer to the paper to spread that paint onto the paper. Also, for variation, cut notches out of the edge of the credit card to spread the paint in stripes.

8. The black writing is rewritten with a white pen, making it more prominent, and then sticker strips of days of the week are added as borders to the sides of the spread. Part of a paper tape measure is collaged at the bottom.

9. Another cut-out tortoise image is collaged down, and more writing is added with a white pen. *Steady as She Goes* is stamped around the newly added tortoise.

10. Another thought balloon with text is written with a yellow pen, and then graphic stamps are added.

PROMPT:
TRASH & TREASURE

It's time to put on the gloves and get serious. We're going to take an inventory and make a trash and treasure list. Turn to a spread in your book and prepare it with gesso. Write or stamp *Trash* at the top of the left page and *Treasure* at the top of the right page. On each page, draw a line down about one-third of the way in.

Now close your eyes and look around. Take a mental inventory of the things in your life that are important and have power or meaning, whether it's good or bad. They can be objects, people, situations, habits, or experiences. Open your eyes and write down the things that are trash—the things that are holding you back, weighing you down, or just not good for you—in the narrow column on the trash side. Put all of the positive and good things in the column on the treasure side.

After making the lists, write about the items on both sides. Why are you holding on to the trash? Why are you afraid to let go of it? What are you doing to celebrate the things on the treasure side? Is there anything you need to do to support it or show more

appreciation? Like give it a cleaning? Move it to a different place? Tell it you love it? Do you have some items, talents, possibilities that have gone unnoticed because they've gotten lost in the clutter?

Now turn to a new spread. Create a trash and treasure journal page that is a visual and written representation of what you gleaned from the writing you just did, how you feel about the items on the lists, and what needs to be done.

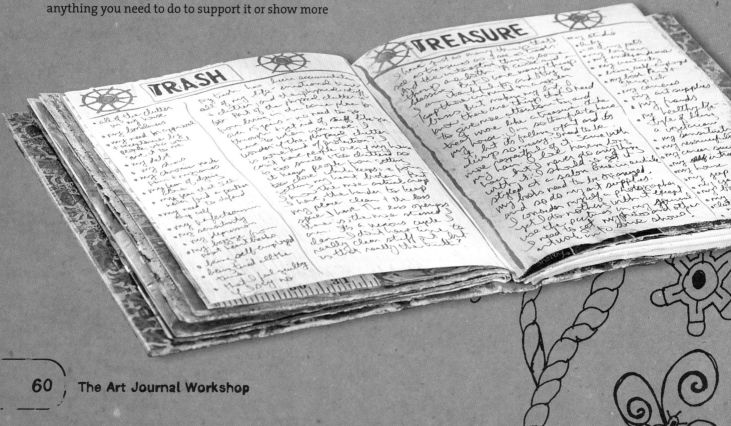

1.

The journal spread before starting

2.

After gesso is applied, *Trash* and *Treasure* are stamped, and then a red marker is used to draw the boxes and column lines. The lists are written with a marker and bulleted with a pink paint pen.

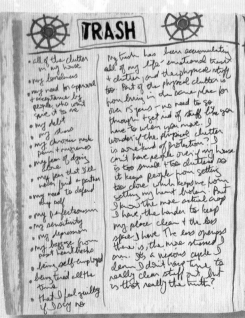

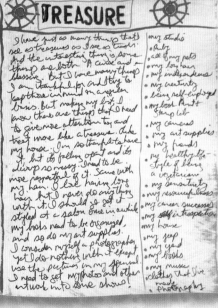

3.

Thoughts are written about the lists with a marker, and then blue lines are added with a brush pen. Stamps are added with blue ink and then embellished with a marker.

4. On a new spread after masking tape is used to cover holes on the Braille page near the spine, gesso is applied, and then brown and yellow paint are rolled on with a brayer.

5. Blue paint is rolled on with a brayer, and then a wash of yellow is painted over the spread.

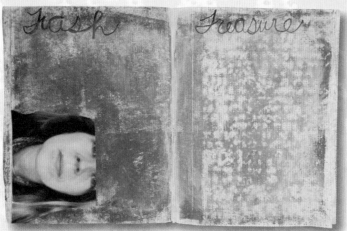

6. The white paint is applied with a paper towel and baby wipe, and then scrubbed off in areas to show the background. After a cut-out self-portrait is collaged down, *Trash* and *Treasure* are written with a brush pen.

7. Words are then added with alphabet stamps. Writing is added with a pen and a marker, and then zipper-printed tape is applied across the spread.

 Workable fixative can be used to seal inkjet prints that aren't printed with waterproof ink, so you can work on top of the print without the ink bleeding.

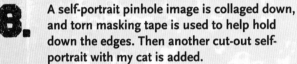

8. A self-portrait pinhole image is collaged down, and torn masking tape is used to help hold down the edges. Then another cut-out self-portrait with my cat is added.

9. Green paint is applied to the masking tape, blending it with the background. Then text is added with alphabet stamps, a pen, and a marker.

10. A handmade oval stamp is stamped for part of a border. Parts of the stamped letters that overlap the self-portrait are outlined with a white pen to help them show up. Pink water-soluble oil pastel is used to add more color to the border and background. A blue pen is used to write back over *Trash* and *Treasure* and to embellish the stamped ovals. More writing is added, and the self-portrait and cat are outlined.

PROMPT:
SILENCE THE CRITIC

In this exercise, we'll have a written conversation and work with our nondominant hand to tap into our unconscious, hidden self. The dominant hand controls and is logical. The nondominant hand taps into the feeling side of the brain, making it easier to cut through to our true desires and get past the practical side and "shoulds."

In this conversation, the nondominant hand represents your heart's desire or a big goal or dream you want to accomplish. The dominant hand represents your block or your critic—the voice that stops you. On a separate piece of paper, start writing a dialogue between these two characters, with your nondominant hand writing about the dream you choose to focus on and your dominant hand answering why it blocks your dream. Go back and forth between the two hands/characters. Because it's harder to write with your nondominant hand, you cut through the extraneous crap and clarify what you want, which creates a shift in your thoughts and perception. Writing with your nondominant hand forces you to slow down and be present.

In your book, make a spread using collage, painting, stamping, and writing that visually represents the positive message from your nondominant hand and how it triumphed over the critic. After you finish, attach the written dialogue in an envelope to the edge of the spread. (See page 30 for more on hinging a piece of ephemera to the edge of a page.)

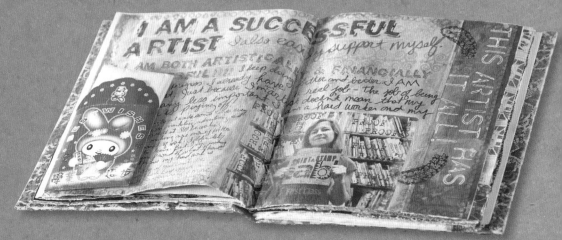

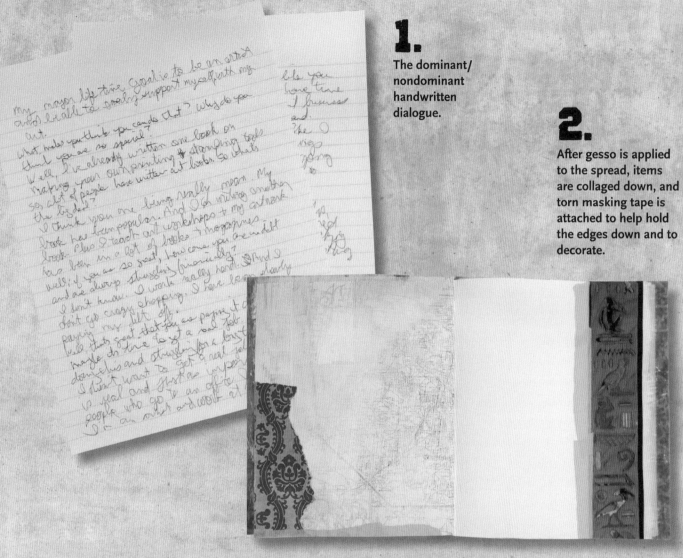

1.
The dominant/
nondominant
handwritten
dialogue.

2.
After gesso is applied
to the spread, items
are collaged down, and
torn masking tape is
attached to help hold
the edges down and to
decorate.

3.
Red paint is applied over
the entire spread with a
brush, and a baby wipe
is used to spread it and
scrub off areas to show
the collaged elements.
Ochre paint is then
applied with a credit card.

4. White paint is applied with a paper towel and scrubbed around with a baby wipe. Words are then added with alphabet stamps and a marker.

5. A photo is collaged, and then more words are added with alphabet stamps.

6. Markers and a pen are used to add more writing, then *Proof* is stamped repeatedly on the photo.

7. A sentence is created with a Dymo label maker and attached to the page, and red paint is buffed over the embossed letters to color them. Words are stenciled with a white pen, and rub-ons are added.

 TIP To use old press type or old rub-ons that don't transfer well or look like they will flake off, cover them with transparent tape after transferring them.

8. A stamp is stamped repeatedly on the spread, and then some of the writing is retraced with a metallic pen and a black pen. A border of circles is drawn with a green marker. A repurposed item that stamps concentric circles is used.

9. Metallic crayons and water-soluble oil pastels are used to add color and scribbles.

10. Transparent tape is used to hinge a decorative envelope to the finished journal spread after the pages of written dialogue are folded and placed inside.

PROMPT:
INTERVENTION

You already know this, but it's time for an intervention. This is your wake-up call. We sometimes do things or have patterns that aren't good for us, which we don't want to admit to ourselves. Only those who care for us the most have the love and strength to be brutally honest because they want to help us on a better path. An intervention is never easy, and we usually don't want to hear it, but we need to. We already know what's going to be said, but we need to hear it from the person who is most important to us so it sinks in and we know it's true. You are that person. You need to be that best friend for yourself.

Start preparing a spread in your journal with gesso, paint, collage, stamps, and whatever else you feel like using. As your hands are busy, let your mind loose to go deep inside to let out what this intervention needs to be about. What would your best friend tell you if they said what you really needed to hear? Since they know you well, what behaviors or patterns have they noticed over a period of time, whether they are old or new?

As it comes to you, start adding words and other elements to express what needs to be done. If you have trouble, do some stream-of-consciousness writing to help you get to the heart of the matter, either directly in your journal or on another piece of paper. Just start writing, asking yourself questions without thinking about it too much, until it comes.

Keep in mind that your best friend will tell it to you in the manner that you need to hear it to get the point. Keep journaling about it until you feel the intervention is over. After some time has passed, if your friend sees you slipping back into your old ways, it might be time to repeat this exercise.

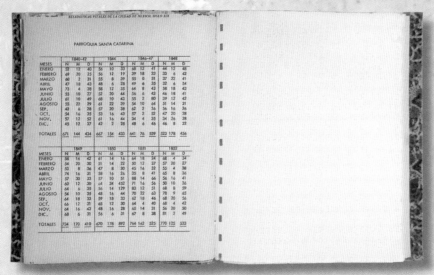

1.

The journal spread
before starting

2.

Torn papers are
collaged down, then
gesso is applied.

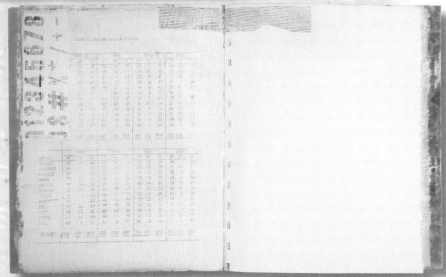

3.

Green paint is applied
with a credit card, then
spread around and
scrubbed with a baby
wipe. Blue paint is applied
with a brush, then
scrubbed off with
a baby wipe to expose
the background and
collaged items.

69

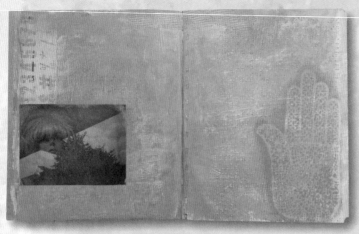

4. Yellow paint is applied through a Mehndi hand stencil. A personal photograph taken while doing "Photo Field Trip," page 88, is torn and cut to a smaller size, then collaged down. Blue paint is applied over the photograph, then scrubbed off, leaving the edges painted.

5. Yellow and green inks are used to color the photograph, and then a cut-out image of a Renaissance painting is collaged down.

6. Words are added with alphabet stamps and a brush pen.

7. The horizontal lines for writing are stamped, and then more words are stamped. Writing is added on the lines with a mini fountain pen, and then a word is corrected with a black marker. Water is applied to the photograph to soften the emulsion, and then it is distressed with a sanding block. Several colors of ink are applied to it.

TIP Concentrated watercolor inks add color to photographs printed in photo labs. See *The Complete Guide to Altered Imagery* by Karen Michel for detailed information.

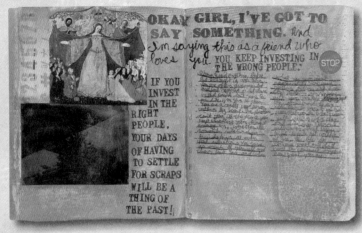

8. A sticker that lost its adhesive is glued down. More words are added with alphabet stamps.

9. A self-portrait PoGo print is attached. Chinese stamps are added. Outlined letters are drawn with a marker and filled in with a red paint pen. Cut-out text from a children's book is collaged down and painted with yellow watercolor to tone down the white background.

10. A doodle stamp is added and embellished with a paint pen. A hand-carved stamp is used to stamp a border. Then a black pen is used to create faux stitching on the personal photos and to write *Together* over the book clipping.

PROMPT: BIG FEAR

We all have something we are afraid of, something that worries us and colors our world and the way we navigate life. It might be something you have never told anyone or something you don't want to admit to yourself. Maybe it's something you are ashamed of or something that might seem silly. Getting it out on paper, even if no one else sees it, sheds light on it. It makes it not so scary or taboo and is a positive step in dealing with the fear to help change it.

On a separate piece of paper, start writing about your big fear. If there are several, start writing about all of them to help focus on the one you want to deal with for this exercise. If you aren't sure what you

fear, just start writing, asking yourself what you are really afraid of. Write without laboring over it, just letting the words come onto the paper. You might be surprised by what bubbles up. Write until you feel you are finished, writing on the back of the page or on a second sheet if necessary.

Then set it aside and create a journal page using paints, collage, stamps, images, and whatever else you like to express your big fear. Journal about or summarize what came up during the writing and what you can start doing about it, even if that is simply writing a positive affirmation. Getting it out will help calm the fear. After you finish, attach the writing you first did to the journal spread, either by itself or in an envelope attached to the edge of the spread. (See page 30 for more on hinging a piece of ephemera to the edge of a page.)

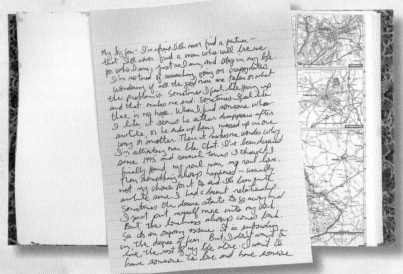

1.

Writing about my big fear is done on a separate sheet of paper.

2.

Torn pieces of decorative paper and a page from an old shorthand book are collaged down.

3.

A thin layer of gesso is applied to the page. Yellow paint is applied with a brush, then scrubbed around with a baby wipe, exposing areas of the background.

4. A wash of red paint is applied, and then areas are removed with a baby wipe.

5. A cut-out self-portrait, taken with a kids' digital camera, is collaged down. Then two kinds of decorative tape are added to the top and bottom of the photo to help meld it with the spread.

6. A vintage photograph is collaged down, and a flower-bouquet sticker is cut and attached to the man's hand. Torn masking tape is applied to the photo's corners. Words are added with alphabet stamps.

7. Writing is added with a brush marker. The horizontal lines for writing are stamped, and then more writing is done on the lines with a marker.

TIP If collaging something across the center of the book, fold it first where it will rest in the spine's middle dip. Attach it starting with the center fold, working out so the piece will conform to the book at the spine, and opening and closing the book won't tear it.

8. A paint pen is used to draw outlined letters, and writing is added with a white pen. Hearts are stamped with a hand-carved stamp. Rub-ons are applied, and then little flowers are drawn with markers. The text in white is written over with a silver paint pen.

9. The spelling of *Loneliness* in the block of text is corrected with a marker, and then the silver text is written over again with a black marker. The outlined letters are filled in with a red marker.

10.

Color is added to the background and vintage photograph with colored pencils. A caption is created with a Dymo label maker and attached. A metallic gold pen is used to outline the stamped hearts, self-portrait, and man. A Chinese envelope is attached with decorative tape after the written page is folded and placed inside. *My Big Fear* is written on the envelope with paint pens.

CALL TO ACTION EXERCISES

T he "Call to Action Exercises" are just that. They are about taking action through specific exercises. You are asked to do certain activities, often outside of the journal, and then come back to your book to document your experience. You'll often create art or work in a journal while sitting down without much physical activity, and also while solitary. These exercises will get you out of the chair and out of the house, which can help get you outside of your head. If there is a reason you can't get out of the house to do these, perhaps you can find a way to change the activity so you can still take action in any manner possible and get the same results. Brainstorm! There is always a solution!

PROMPT: TAKE ACTION

T his "Call to Action Exercise" is perfect when you are stuck in a rut or feeling lethargic. When you begin to feel down or edgy, making a game plan and physically doing something, regardless of what it is, will help you to feel better and get motivated. Taking action allows you to be in control of your life, which is empowering. In this journaling exercise, you'll write about how you are feeling and make a list of activities you can do right then to get you off that couch or to lift your spirits and give you an attitude change.

Open your book to a new spread. Go ahead and prepare it however you'd like, such as painting on a layer of gesso and adding some collage and paint. Then start writing about how you feel and perhaps why you are feeling that way. While you are doing

that, make a list of at least five things you can easily do right then or a little later (such as taking a walk or cooking something good to eat) that involve movement to shift your mood or energy level. It really doesn't matter what it is or how big or little the activity is, but make it simple enough that you can accomplish it in a short period of time. Finish off the pages with any embellishing you'd like to add. After you are done working in your journal, go do the activities on your list! If you choose, after you finish, journal about how taking action made you feel. For me, just working in my journal to make my list makes me start to feel much better. Do this exercise whenever you start to get that humdrum feeling.

1.
The journal spread
before starting

2.
After a thin layer of
gesso is applied, scraps
of wrapping paper and
part of an incense box
are collaged down.
Masking tape is added
to the end of the
incense box to help
hold it down.

3.
A layer of blue paint is
applied over the whole
page and collaged pieces,
then scrubbed down with
a baby wipe.

4. Green and yellow are painted on top of the blue.

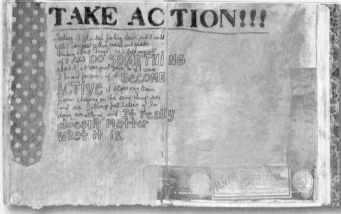

5. Text is added with alphabet stamps and a marker.

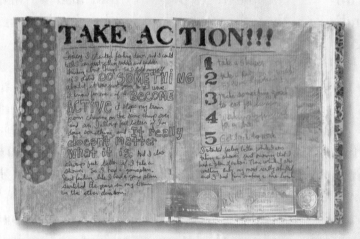

6. I made my list of activities using a gel pen and rubber stamps, then did more writing.

7. The spread is embellished with rubber stamps and "urgent" tape, and the outlined letters are colored in with a marker.

 If anything tears as you are working, it can be fixed! Simply collage on top of it, add some masking tape, or just add more paint on top if it. Be sure the surface is dry before doing any of these tricks to fix.

8. A cut-out PoGo print and another picture are added and an orange paint marker is used to add circles on some of the stamped images.

9. Circles are stenciled on with orange paint and pencils, and then some of the circles are outlined with an orange paint pen.

10. Red circles are stamped with a pencil eraser. *Take Action* and outlined words were outlined in red to make them more prominent. Several colors of water-soluble oil pastels and crayons add more colors and scribbles.

PROMPT:
DO YOUR JOY

Before you can do your joy, you need to do the exercise, "Document Your Joy," on page 108. After that, choose an activity from your joy list and actually do it! Then in your book, create an art journal spread about your experience. Use paint, collage, writing, and any other items to express how you felt while doing something you love to do. If you took any photos during the activity or did some drawing, use those in the spread. Joyful activities help fill the well of your soul, so to speak, and journaling about them creates a positive visual reminder for you to do them regularly. In my journal for this exercise, I attached actual pieces of the fabric that I over-dyed and used to make my skirt and made notes about what worked and what to change on the next skirt.

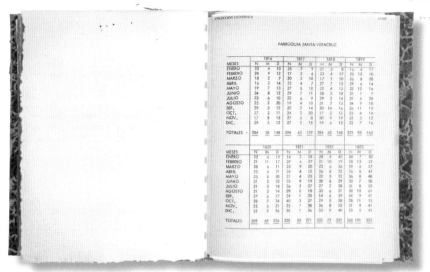

1.

The journal spread before starting.

2.

A thin layer of gesso is applied to the pages.

3.

A self-portrait I took wearing the skirt I made is torn to size and collaged down. Then scraps of the fabric I over-dyed and used in the skirt are also collaged.

4. Words are added with alphabet stamps.

5. Horizontal lines for writing are added with a stamp.

6. A wash of red paint is applied over the exposed gesso, part of the photo, and edges of the fabric to tie everything together. The outlined stamped letters are filled in with a blue marker.

7. Writing is added with a marker, and then more lines for writing are stamped.

8. More text is added with a marker, a blue pen, and alphabet stamps.

9. The first sentence of the writing is written over with a white pen to make it easier to read. A handmade stamp is used to faintly stamp buttons onto the fabric. Dymo labelmaker tape is added, and then a rub-on of stitching is applied.

Markers, crayons, glitter glue, and water-soluble oil pastels are used to add more color and sparkle. Circles are stamped with a pencil eraser. A red pen is used for drawing a border and outlining the flowers on the fabric.

PROMPT:
USE IT OR LOSE IT

Speaking from personal experience, as creative people we tend to gather and "collect" various art supplies and mixed-media items to use. Everything is eye candy, and we have to have whatever is the flavor of the month. But it builds up, gets put in the back of the drawer or shelves, and after a while, we don't know what we have, which means it doesn't get used. It adds to our clutter. Then we spend more time looking for things than we do making art.

Before you go buy that next art supply, stamp, or tube of paint, do this exercise. It's a great one to do multiple times to use things you already have and to help you decide what things need new homes. When I did this, I was amazed by what I found and things I was reintroduced to. Who knew I had all that?

Get a small box or something to collect items in. Dig through your supplies, tools, and stashes, gathering things you haven't used in a very long time. (Don't go crazy—you can use only so much to create a journal page.) Now work in your journal, using these forgotten items, journaling about anything you want, or select any of the journaling prompts in this chapter. When I did this, I used only items I gathered for the exercise, other than basic materials like gesso, glue, brushes, and so on.

After you finish, decide what you liked using and want to keep and what to set free. For me, with some of the items it was like reconnecting with old friends. With others it was deciding to say goodbye. Those items can be sold on eBay or Etsy, swapped with friends, or donated to charities and organizations such as women's shelters, youth programs, and senior centers. Check your area to find out what organizations would like these items.

TIP Get together with some friends to do this exercise. Then when you are finished, swap unwanted items. You'll have fun, make art with friends, and swap for new stuff. The stash is always greener on the other side.

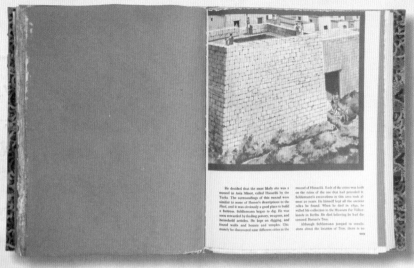

1.

The journal spread
before starting

2.

After a layer of gesso is
applied, pink paint is
rolled on with a brayer.

3.

Yellow paint is applied
with a brayer.

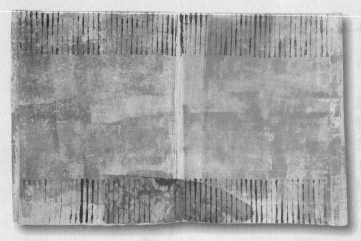

4. Washes of yellow and blue paint are added with a brush. Torn paper is collaged down. Corrugated paper and blue paint are used to print the border.

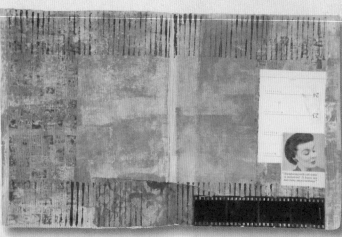

5. A background stamp is applied to the sides with a nonpermanent stamp pad. More items are collaged down. A film negative is attached and stapled at the bottom.

6. Various ephemera and stickers are added. The film negative and Timesavers sticker are distressed with a sanding block. Paint is added to the negative and buffed off. A wash of several colors of paint is applied to some elements to blend them with the background.

7. Pink then yellow paint is added to some of the newly collaged items and scrubbed off with baby wipes, removing the left border. A self-portrait is collaged down, and then decorative tape is attached to help hold down the bottom edge. A cut-out illustration from a children's book is collaged down. Words are stamped with alphabet stamps.

TIP When I work in a book, often the stapler won't reach where I want to attach. If I still want the staples as embellishments, I staple the item by itself and then glue the item into the journal.

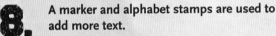

8. A marker and alphabet stamps are used to add more text.

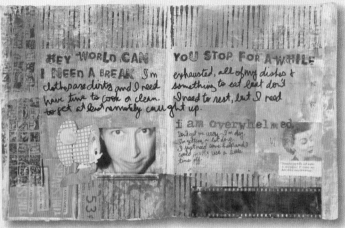

9. More writing is added with an old, worn-out marker, then written over with a pen. *Really* is emphasized with a white pen. Blue paint is used to stamp a background stamp along the side.

10. White paint is used to stamp a clock stamp, and then white lines are drawn with a pen. A Speed Demon sticker is attached, then distressed with a sanding block. Several colors of metallic oil pastels are applied to add more colors and also to soften the top edge of the self-portrait, then blended with a finger.

PROMPT:
PHOTO FIELD TRIP

This is a fun, multistep Call to Action that involves getting out, shopping, and walking around taking pictures—all before the journaling starts! If you don't have enough time to do it all in the same day, you might want to break it down, completing different steps as you have time. I did it all in the same day, and it felt decadent to have that much creative fun all grouped together.

➡ Go on a search for an inexpensive, plastic camera that uses film. Check thrift stores, garage sales, or even dollar stores. If you can't find one, a disposable camera that uses film will work. But for me, hunting for cheap plastic cameras is half the fun of using them. I lucked out and found so many cheap cameras at the Salvation Army, I had to limit myself to three (but I used only two for the exercise). I think I spent around $5 for all three of them!

Then get some film for the camera if you don't already have some. (Film will probably cost more than the cheap camera unless you also find some at the thrift store or dollar store.)

➡ Go out and take pictures of whatever you want and use the whole roll of film. Have fun! Take close-up shots and try different angles. Take a self-portrait or two. The purpose here is to get out and be active and to look at things in a new way or that perhaps you never noticed before. I love to walk around my downtown alleys taking pictures, or to photograph everyday things that normally go unnoticed.

➡ Drop the film off somewhere that will process it in an hour or so, if possible. While you are waiting, go look at kids' art supplies that you might like to use and get some. Also check out the clearance section of craft and art supplies. The purpose here isn't to go crazy buying new supplies but to treat yourself to several inexpensive things you might not normally try. I found some paint in colors I normally wouldn't use (but ended up loving), some stickers, rub-ons, and tissue paper.

➡ When your photos are done, go make a journal page playing with your new supplies and photos. Journal about your experience, whether you liked it, why you photographed what you did, and so on. If you'd like to have more room, attach another page to create a three-page spread (see "Creating a Three-Page Spread," page 42). The leftover photos can be used in some of the other journaling exercises.

Plastic cameras purchased at a thrift store

Thrift store plastic cameras and the photos taken with them

1.

A thin layer of gesso is applied to the pages.

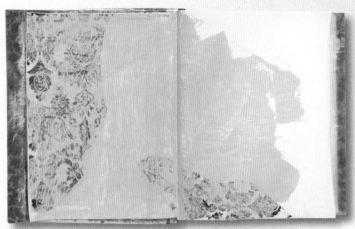

2. Tissue paper is torn then collaged. Lavender paint is applied with a credit card.

3. Orange, more lavender, and blue paint are applied in layers with a baby wipe and scrubbed off in areas to reveal the colors and textures underneath.

4. Personal photos taken during the field trip are chosen and collaged down after one is torn to a smaller size.

5. Decorative tape is applied to some edges of the photos. More lavender paint is added around the photos and on the tape with a finger and brush, then scrubbed off in areas with a baby wipe. Alphabet stamps and markers are used to add the words.

6. A marker is used to fill in the outlined letters. Lines and circles are drawn with a gold metallic pen between the columns of writing. Stickers and a rub-on are applied.

7. A pink water-soluble oil pastel is colored around the photos and border, then blended into the background with a finger. Colored inks are added onto the black and white photos. An orange water-soluble oil pastel is used to add more color, then blended with a finger. The stamped letters are outlined with a gold pen.

8. Circles are stenciled with a marker to create a border. A red pen is used to write over the first sentence for emphasis and to outline again the drawn words at the bottom. Several crayons are used to add more colors and scribbles. Another sticker is attached.

Affirmation flyers and magnets
placed around downtown

PROMPT:
URBAN
AFFIRMATION ART

My friend, Bobbi Studstill, used to make small, one-of-a-kind cards that she called *Rebel Art Cards*. They were a cross between a business card and an artist trading card. She would leave them around in places such as art gallery openings and other public events for people to find. I always loved the idea and was excited by the prospect of combining them with visual affirmations. They seemed a perfect union. And the affirmation art could take various forms: stickers, magnets, or little flyers, released into the public for strangers to discover just when they needed a lift. For this exercise, the original art is created in the journal, scanned, and then printed in multiples onto regular paper or sticker paper (full-sheet labels) for distribution.

To get started, make a list of general affirmations you would like to turn into little pieces of art. For example, some of mine are "Be your own superhero!" and "I love and accept myself exactly the way I am." Decide the size you want the original artwork to be, noting that when scanned it can be enlarged or reduced before printing. I had old business card magnets that I wanted to use, so mine were in proportion to the magnets. (Full sheets of magnets, available in craft stores, can also be used and cut to any size.) Cut a cardboard template the desired size of each affirmation art, and then trace around it in your journal, putting several on each page.

Don't get too close to the spine, because it might be hard to scan if the book doesn't lie flat. Create the visual affirmations using whatever materials you want. If desired, include your email address, website, or contact information on the card.

Scan the finished affirmations, print them on regular paper or full-sheet labels if you want them to be stickers, or take your journal to a copy shop and have it copied there. I scanned mine, then used a layout program to put as many as I could fit onto a page without any space between, making them easier to cut out. I used two different affirmations per sheet and was able to put five of each one on the page (ten total). I also printed some larger ones on regular paper to place around as flyers.

If you are making magnets, either with adhesive magnet sheets or by using a magnet cartridge in a Xyron machine, the affirmations can be printed on regular paper instead of sticker paper. Since my magnets weren't adhesive, I printed them on sticker paper, cut them apart, and then attached to the magnets.

After the affirmations are printed, cut out, and attached to magnets if desired, place them around public areas like coffee shops and bookstores. Flyers can also be placed on telephone poles, and magnets can be placed anywhere the magnet will hold on, even outside! I had just as much fun releasing my Urban Affirmation Art as I did making it. After distributing them, write on the affirmation journal spread about your experience.

1.

A thin layer of gesso is applied to the journal spread, and then the cardboard template is made and traced to outline the working area. A list of affirmations is made on a separate piece of paper.

2.

Various borders are collaged with paper. Watercolor and paint are applied to create the different backgrounds.

3.

A cut-out copy of my superhero drawing is collaged, and words are added with a pen, marker, and alphabet stamps. A hand-carved stamp is used to create a star border. The stamped letters are outlined with a metallic pen. Rub-ons are added as a border, and a star is drawn with metallic pens for the superhero. The stamped stars are filled in with a gold pen.

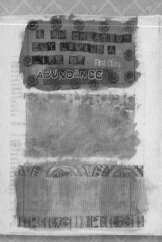

4. An acceptance affirmation is written with a marker. A hand-carved stamp is added, then outlined with pens. Pens and paint pens are used to embellish. Watercolor pencils and paint are used to color the background. A red pen is used to write over the affirmation.

5. Crayons are used to add color to the awesome affirmation. A red pen is used to circle the stamped stars, then outline the superhero letters. An abundance affirmation is stamped, and then *Abundance* is outlined with a white pen. A yellow paint wash is used to color in the stamped letters. *First Class* is stamped. A hand-carved starburst stamp is used to create the border.

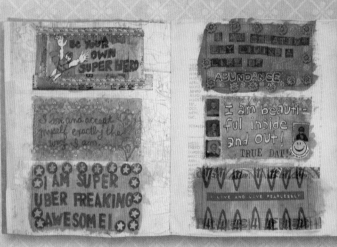

6. The starburst stamps are outlined with a yellow paint pen. Different colors of water-soluble oil pastels and neon pens are used to add color and embellishments. A strip of vintage photos is collaged to a new piece, then covered with transparent pink tape. Words are drawn and stamped.

7. The outlined letters are filled in with a yellow pen, then outlined again with a marker. Another vintage photo and smiley face are collaged down. Pens are used to add smiles, outline *True dat!*, outline the single photo, and draw a border. A Dymo label maker is used to create the last affirmation. A hand-carved stamp is used for the border.

8. Various pens are used to embellish the last piece. Yellow paint is applied to the embossed letters, then buffed off to color them. Printed clippings with my website address are collaged onto each piece. Watercolor is used to color those paper pieces, blending them into the background.

9. The artwork is scanned, then printed onto paper and full-sheet labels for flyers, stickers, and magnets. They are cut out, and then some stickers are applied to the business card magnets.

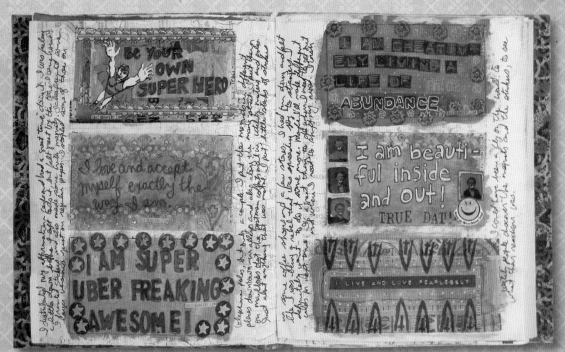

10. After distributing the affirmations in public places, writing about the experience is added to the spread.

PROMPT:
MAIL ART GESTURE

This idea for a "Call to Action" came about when I thought of the importance of small gestures. We often overlook the everyday small gestures that slowly build bonds and keep us connected with each other. Sure, we are all busy with our own personal struggles and challenges, but why not make small creative gestures on a regular basis to reconnect or keep in touch with someone? You'll enjoy doing it, and they'll appreciate knowing that not only were you thinking of them, you also took the time to make them a piece of art.

For this exercise, our small gesture will be manifested in the form of mail art! Mail art is a little piece of double-sided art that is sent through the mail. I prefer my mail art to travel without a package or envelope. I like to send it off as it is—brave and bold without protection so that whatever happens to it along the way becomes part of the piece. Every hand that touches it and every eye that sees it on its journey becomes part of its life. Those hands and eyes are the patrons in the gallery. Don't deny any potential viewers that fun experience!

Mail art can be mixed-media work combining collage, stamping, painting, and anything else you want to include. It's a great way to try out new materials or techniques on a small scale without having to commit to a big project. Plus it doesn't take any special tools, materials, or skill level. You can make mail art from things you already have around the house. And even someone with little or no art experience can have fun making art.

My mail art is often made from recycled packaging cardboard such as cereal and frozen pizza boxes. The backing cardboard from sticker packages and similar items is also great—it serves a double purpose because it already has that little hanger on the top, making it easier for the lucky recipient to hang it after they get it in the mail.

Think about a friend whom you haven't taken time for or heard from lately or whose phone call you didn't yet get around to returning. Using salvaged cardboard for the base, create a mail art card for that person using any images of the friend or the two of you if you have them. Think of this as a small, double-sided journal page. Write about a fond memory and let the friend know you are thinking of them. Leave room to write the address and be sure everything is attached really well. When it's ready for the mail, be sure to take it to the post office to find out how much postage it needs. It may require a little more than a regular postcard. While you're at it, make several to reconnect with more than one friend!

1. The cereal box is flattened, then cut to the desired size with scissors. Near the top a packaging hanger is attached with glue and staples. Masking tape is used to cover the backs of the staples and to help ensure that the hanger is completely attached.

3. The other side is covered with overlapping rows of masking tape.

2. The printed side is collaged with tissue paper, and the edges are folded over to the other side.

4. Several layers of paint are applied and scrubbed down over the masking tape and hanger, creating an aged look and revealing the texture.

5. A copy of a Polaroid transfer of my friend's house, made during a visit, is torn to size and collaged down.

6. Several layers of paint are applied and scrubbed down over the tissue paper, showing the printing and various colors. An enlarged copy of a photo-booth picture of the two of us is collaged down.

7. A wash of yellow paint is applied to the edges of the photo, tying it in with the background. A letter to my friend is added with alphabet stamps and marker.

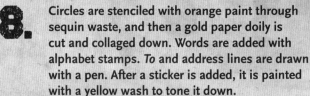

8. Circles are stenciled with orange paint through sequin waste, and then a gold paper doily is cut and collaged down. Words are added with alphabet stamps. *To* and address lines are drawn with a pen. After a sticker is added, it is painted with a yellow wash to tone it down.

9. A hand-carved stamp is used along the top and bottom. Circles are stamped with a pencil eraser on the sides and hanger. Writing is added with a marker. Pens and crayons are used for outlining and adding color. A rub-on is added. A repurposed item that stamps concentric circles is used.

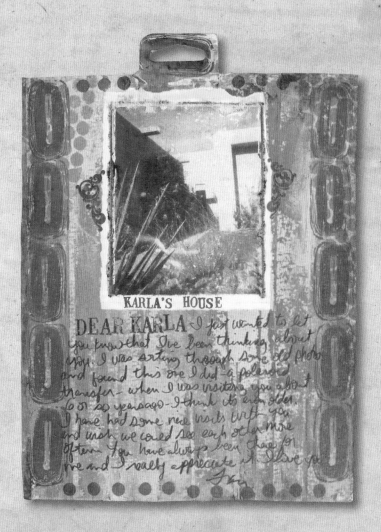

10.

Circles are stenciled with orange paint through sequin waste, and then a hand-carved stamp is added along the sides and hanger. Rub-ons are applied to the sides of the photo, then a pencil eraser is used to stamp circles along the top and bottom.

SELF-CARE EXERCISES

This section has exercises and projects dealing specifically with ways to artistically nurture and care for yourself. These projects can help boost your emotional state in times of need or be supportive while you tackle challenging tasks or situations. Most of the exercises are worked directly in your book, and a few involve creating cards. As with the other sections, they combine mixed-media materials with writing for personal expression and development.

PROMPT: CHECKING IN

Frequently we get so busy, we don't take the time to check in with ourselves to see what's going on or how we feel. Just stopping to allow ourselves this time to be present with our emotions and work in our journal is wonderful self-care. It might not seem like it, but done on a regular basis, it can make a difference and also help us to be more self-aware. Whether you are feeling positive or a little down, it's still good to see where you are and to get it down in your book; often that will help you to see what you need to do in your life, whether it's taking an action or shifting your outlook. And if the feelings are positive, you'll feel even better if you write and create a journal spread about them.

Open your book to a blank spread. Sit quietly with yourself, being open and listening to what your body, mind, and heart are telling you. If you aren't sure exactly how you feel, go ahead and get started preparing the pages with gesso, collage, and paint. It's okay if you don't know what you are going to journal about. Your busy hands will distract your mind, and soon the feelings and thoughts will show themselves to you. If you still have trouble after you have gotten the pages started, ask yourself some simple questions, as if someone else were interviewing you. If you are still feeling blocked, start writing about it in your book. For example, "I'm feeling stressed out and don't really know why." Sometimes just beginning will get things started. As you are writing and adding images, paint, and embellishments, be open to resolutions or solutions to your situation. If you are journaling about something positive, be open to ways to keep moving in that blissful direction.

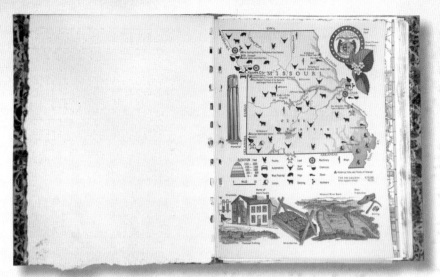

1.

The journal spread before starting

2.

After a thin layer of gesso is applied, text is added with alphabet stamps and a marker.

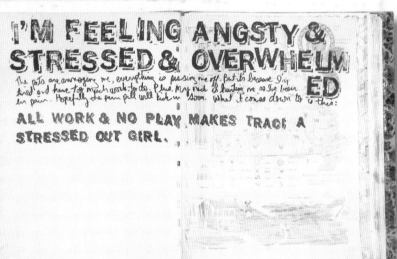

3.

Photos and part of an old book page are collaged down.

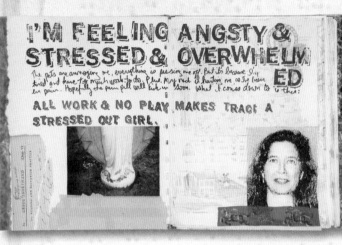

4. Yellow masking tape and a strip from some Joss paper are added.

5. A wash of fluid acrylic is painted over the whole page, including the images. Then an image from incense packaging is added. The edges of it are taped down with masking tape to ensure it is completely attached.

6. The masking tape is painted to meld it with the background, then paint is applied to the outer edges of the spread to create a border.

7. Writing is added about a solution to the stress I was feeling.

8. A Ganesh sticker is applied, and a red paint marker is used to draw lines around the entire edge of the paper.

9. The blue writing is written over with black to make it more legible, and *Hey Ganesh, I need you!* is outlined, then colored in.

10.

A hand-carved stamp is stamped around the photo of the statue, and then a pencil is used to draw circles, filling in some areas. Several colors of watercolor crayons and water-soluble oil pastels are used to add more colors and scribbles.

PROMPT: NURTURE LIST

Self-nurturing is really important to our physical and spiritual well-being. Sometimes we feel guilty if we nurture ourselves, thinking we are being selfish. And when we're busy, it's the first thing to go out the window. We suffer for it later. We need to love ourselves enough to realize how important it is to nurture ourselves on a regular basis. It's great when others nurture us, but in the long run, we need to do it for ourselves before we can do it for, or accept it from, someone else. We deserve it, and we have to believe that we deserve it.

Turn to a spread in your book. Apply a thin layer of gesso or color the page with some pastels before applying the gesso to tint it. On the left page, write a letter to yourself about why you deserve to be nurtured, how important it is, and how much you love yourself. Then on the right page, make a list of the ways you can nurture yourself and write about why you like each item. If you run out of room, attach another page or a card to the edge to continue.

Whenever I start to feel down and want to stop myself before I get down any farther, I turn to my nurture list and start doing the things on it to pull myself out of it. It works! They can even be simple things like burning incense or listening to energetic music and dancing around like a maniac.

1.

The journal spread before starting.

2.

Chalk pastels are scribbled onto the pages.

3.

Gesso is applied over the pastels, blending the colors and tinting the gesso.

4. A nurturing letter is written with markers.

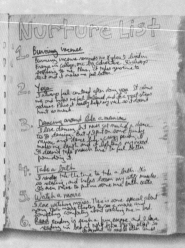

5. A "nurture list" is made with blue and black pens and a black marker.

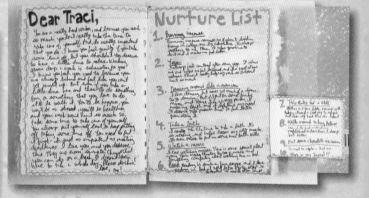

6. The back of a photograph is collaged with an old book page to create more writing area, and then a layer of gesso is applied to it. The photo is attached to the edge of the page with clear tape. The list is continued on the back of the photograph.

7. The outlined letters and numbers are filled in with a pink paint pen. *Dear Traci* is outlined again with a blue pen, and then a border is drawn with pens and markers.

8. Blue and yellow watercolor crayons are dipped in water, then applied to the page to add color. They are smeared with my finger and a wet paintbrush to give more of a watercolor effect.

9. Different colors of crayons are applied for more color and scribbles. A yellow paint pen is used to draw circles.

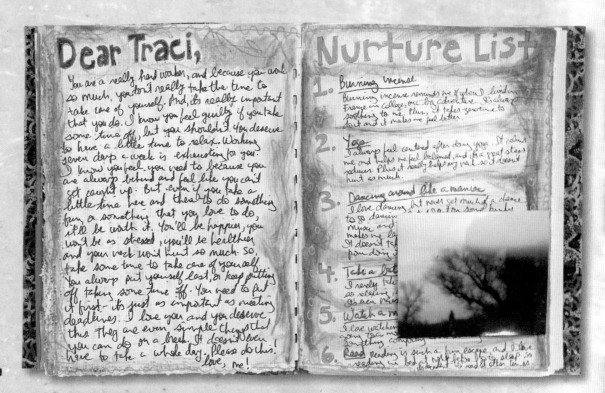

10. The journal spread with the attachment folded in, showing the photograph.

PROMPT:
DOCUMENT YOUR JOY

This Self-Care exercise creates a visual reminder of the things that bring joy to your life. Not only will it be fun to create, but then when you are in a slump, you can look at your documented joy for a pick-me-up. Also, when we go through a busy period in life, sometimes we need to be reminded of the things that make us happy so we can slow down and get back to them.

Make a list of at least ten things that make you happy and bring you joy. These can include activities, objects, pets, or people. Gather images, words, and phrases that represent the items on your list by searching through your stash and magazines. Alternatively, go on an outing to take pictures. You can also do drawings. The images don't have to be literal but can be anything that suggests the item or activity.

After you've collected the collage items, attach another page to a spread in your book to make a three-page spread. (See "Creating a Three-Page Spread," page 42.) Using the images you have

gathered along with paint, stamps, and any other mixed-media materials, create a collage as a way to document your joy. Write about each item, why it makes you happy, and any other thoughts you have about it. Embellish the elements as desired, working until you feel you are done.

As part of the journaling process, create a decorative page with your list on the back of the attached page when it's folded in. Add some writing about whatever came up while you were collecting the images, thinking about what brings you joy, or creating the journal collage.

1.
The journal spread with a third page attached

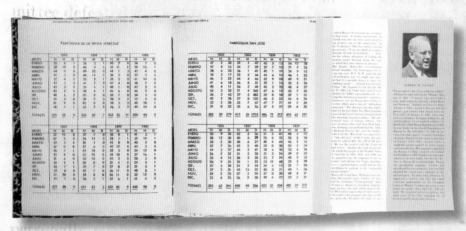

2.
After the spread is prepped with gesso, blue paint is applied with a credit card and spread with a baby wipe. A layer of green paint is added with a paint brush and scrubbed around with a baby wipe to expose the color underneath. A joy list is temporarily written with marker.

3.
Magazine images, the word *Art*, personal photos, and a self-portrait are cut out and collaged down, overlapping in areas.

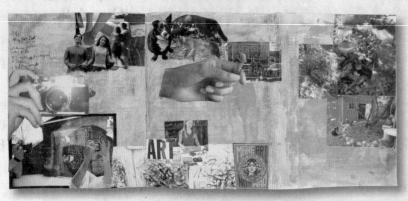

4.

More personal photos and magazine images are cut out and collaged down.

5.

More images are added to the collage, and several photos of my head are cut out and collaged onto bodies from magazine photos, implying that I am doing those activities.

6.

The remaining exposed joy list is covered with background paint. A cut-out drawing that I did of a skirt is collaged down, and then a sewing machine rub-on is applied. A magazine clipping of the word *Happiness* is collaged near the center.

7.

A pen is used to title each activity or item on the collage, and then writing is added about why it brings me joy. Another pen is used to write back over the titles, making them more prominent. *Joy* is outlined, filled in with a pink paint pen, and then outlined again with a black pen.

8.

An orange water-soluble oil pastel is used to draw around the outer edge and then smeared. Various pens are used to embellish the collage. Hand-carved stamps add a border and lines. Decorative tape is applied on the knitting area over some of the cut edges and then painted to tone it down.

9. After the attached page is folded in, a thin layer of gesso and then blue paint are applied. A title is added with alphabet stamps.

10.

My joy list is written with a marker, writing lines are added with a stamp, and then writing is done about how I felt while doing this exercise. The page is embellished with a pink pen, hand-carved stamps, and crayons.

PROMPT:
YOU ARE A LEGEND

If you just physically pretend on a regular basis, no matter how silly it may seem, that "it" is yours, that your life has already taken off, and that you've found true happiness, a tipping point will be reached, stars will be realigned, and new acquaintances will start insisting, "I don't know why, but you look really familiar..."

And, it'll be because their inner eyes already see the legend you are to become.

—from *Notes from the Universe* by Mike Dooley
©www.tut.com

Open your journal to a fresh spread or one you have already prepped. Create a journal spread combining pictures, writing, collage, paint, and stamps to convey the legend that you are to become. However, write as if it has already happened. You are already a legend! If you have a picture of yourself, you can use that as a starting point. If you don't, draw yourself or find images that represent the qualities of your awesomeness. Remember, the imagery doesn't have to be literal—it can simply convey the feeling. Make the spread as awesome as you are. Add glitter glue and embellishments to show what a legend you are! Keep adding text or images as thoughts and ideas occur to you.

1.
The journal spread
before starting

2.
A thin layer of gesso is
applied to the pages.

3.
Yellow paint is applied
with a brush, and then
orange is added with a
credit card and scrubbed
around with a baby wipe.

 Magazine images of crowds are cut out, torn, and collaged down. A wash of orange paint is applied to the images to blend them with the page.

5. A cut-out self-portrait, taken with the built-in camera on my laptop, is collaged down.

 Words are added with alphabet stamps and magazine clippings.

7. Writing about my legend, written as if it has already happened, is done with a marker.

8. More words are added with alphabet stamps, markers, and pens.

9. A black marker is used to write over some words to make them more legible. Outlined words and the stamped headline are filled in with a pen and marker. *Celebrity* is collaged to my neck. More exclamations coming from the crowd are added with a white pen. A yellow pen is used to outline my self-portrait.

10.

Various pens and crayons are used to add color, draw a border, and embellish. Rubber stamps are also added.

PROMPT:
BE SELECTIVE

You are selective about so many things in your life—what you wear, what you eat, where you live, and whom you spend time with. It's all part of who you are and what you want. Often, without realizing it, when you are down or when times are tough, you can entertain and focus on negative thoughts and let them pull you in the wrong direction. Your thoughts are what truly shape who you are and give you a specific kind of life. It's time to start being selective about your thoughts and when they are negative, learn how to turn them around.

Prepare a journal spread with gesso and maybe some paint. Then directly in your journal on the left page, start writing down the core negative thoughts you

have, the various ways your thoughts are hurting you, and how you need to be pickier about them. You can do this with a marker or pen or whatever you choose to write with.

Then reread your nondiscriminatory thoughts and on the right page, turn those negative thoughts into positive affirmations. Do that by changing a negative thought to a positive one and writing it on the page. Write it big so that it's a bold statement. Or stamp it with alphabet stamps. Decorate it with images, stamps, and color to reflect the positive feeling. The images and things you add to the page don't need to be a literal representation but merely evoke the feeling you want to express. You can have several affirmations on the same page.

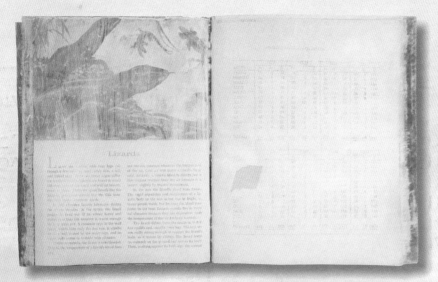

1.

A thin layer of gesso is applied to the page. Masking tape covers a tear made while applying gesso.

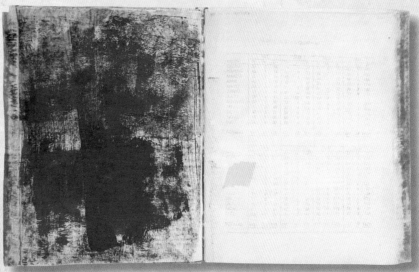

2.

Blue then red paint is rolled on with a brayer.

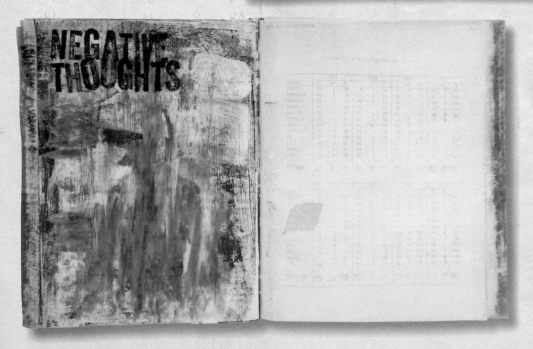

3.

White paint is applied with a credit card before the red paint is completely dry, causing streaks. Words are added with alphabet stamps.

4. My negative thoughts are stamped with alphabet stamps, and then writing about these thoughts is added with a marker.

5. Hand-carved rubber stamps are added to the page. A metallic marker, then white pen, is used to outline the stamped letters. Yellow paint is applied to the right page with a brush and with a baby wipe.

6. Tissue paper and a torn piece of Joss paper are collaged down, and then yellow paint is applied over them with a baby wipe. An image cut out from a candy bar wrapper is collaged down. Words are added with alphabet stamps and written several times with different pens for emphasis.

7. The outlined stamped letters are filled in with a marker. More words are added with a brush pen and alphabet stamps.

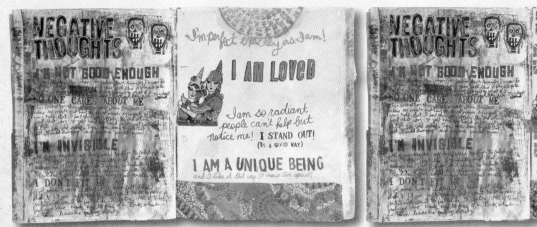

8. The new affirmation is written over with a pen to make it bolder. Then another affirmation is added with alphabet stamps and a pen.

9. A hand-carved stamp is used to create a border. Decorative tape is applied over the bottom edge of the cut-out illustration. A pen is used to embellish the stamped stars.

10. A hand-carved stamp creates a line between two affirmations. More writing is added with a pen. Pens, markers, and water-soluble oil pastels are used to embellish and add more color.

PROMPT: COMMITMENT CARDS

This exercise is to help lay the foundation for making positive changes in your life by committing to regularly work on small things that will make your life better. You will create "commitment cards" that are positive, visual reminders of your commitments.

Prepare a spread in your book with gesso and paint. Write directly in your book to figure out what changes you want to make or actions you want to take on a regular basis. Leave some space to make a list of those changes. These commitments don't have to be time consuming. They can be something that takes only fifteen to twenty minutes, such as meditating or going for a walk. They can be small steps that bring joy into your life not only because of the results but also because you are doing something for yourself and standing by your commitment. After you finish writing, make a commitment list.

Choose the top items from your list. Using cardboard, cut a card for each commitment to any size you want. They don't even all have to be the same size. But don't make them too big in case you want to carry them in your purse or bag. Instead of cutting them out first, you can also work on big pieces of cardboard, painting and collaging both sides so that all of the cards will be unified. After designing the large background piece, cut out the cards and work on each one individually.

Collage, paint, stamp, and write on them to be a visual reminder of your commitments. The cards can be set out where you can see them, or you can carry them with you as reminders.

You can choose specific cards for each day and alternate them. Each day renew your commitments to yourself and forgive yourself if you weren't able to keep them.

1.

After a thin layer of gesso is applied to the page, lavender paint is put on with a brush.

2.

The heading is outlined, then filled in with a marker. The writing is added with a marker. After a box is drawn with a brush marker, the list is made with alphabet stamps and a pen.

3.

The spread is decorated with stamps, pens, crayons, water-soluble oil pastels, and a sticker.

4. Two pieces of cardboard are cut from food packaging. The printed sides are covered with patterned tissue paper, then thin layers of orange and mustard paint. The other sides are layered with two different decorative tapes. Next, both pieces are cut into four pieces roughly the same size, making eight pieces total.

5. A personal photograph is collaged, and then decorative tape is applied to the sides. Words are added with alphabet stamps. Pens are used for embellishing.

6. A thin layer of lavender paint is applied and scrubbed. Then words are added with alphabet stamps. A pen, marker, and colored pencils are used for embellishing, and circles are stamped with a pencil eraser.

7. A hand-carved stamp is used for the border. A pen is used to draw *Meditate*, which is filled in with a marker. Another hand-carved stamp is applied. Pens are used for doodling.

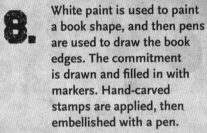

8. White paint is used to paint a book shape, and then pens are used to draw the book edges. The commitment is drawn and filled in with markers. Hand-carved stamps are applied, then embellished with a pen.

9. A hand-carved stamp of a yoga position is stamped, then *Yoga* is drawn with a pen. Other stamps are applied, and then a pen is used for outlining.

10. A cut-out magazine image is collaged down. After words are added with alphabet stamps, a border is drawn with pens.

11. A personal photo is torn to size and collaged down, and then words are added with a pen and alphabet stamps. The outlined letters are filled in with a marker, and the stamped letters are outlined with a pen. A border is made with a stamp and pencil eraser, then embellished with pens.

12. A moldable foam stamp is used in the center, and then a border is drawn with a pen. Words are added with alphabet stamps. A game piece and pen are used to trace circles for the sides. A pen is used to outline the stamped letters and the lace stamp. Dots are made inside the circles with an orange paint pen.

RESOURCES

Many of the materials used in this book can be found locally in hobby stores, craft stores, art supply stores, or discount dollar stores, if you don't already have them. Here is a list of some sources for mail order, as well as inspirational books and links. Also, please visit my website for more information and to see more of my work.

MATERIALS

Traci Bunkers/Bonkers Handmade Originals
workshops, rubber stamp and mixed-media supplies, handmade journals, do-it-yourself kits
www.TraciBunkers.com
P.O. Box 442099
Lawrence, KS 66044

CARAN d'ACHE
paints, pens, pastels, watercolor crayons, and pencils
www.carandache.com

Copic Marker
paper, sketchbooks, and markers
www.copicmarker.com

cute tape
Japanese Washi tape, Korean deco tape, stickers, and stationery
www.cutetape.com

Daniel Smith, Inc.
papers and art supplies
www.danielsmith.com

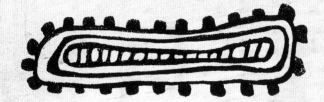

Dick Blick Art Materials
art and craft supplies
www.dickblick.com

DYMO
Dymo label makers
www.dymo.com

FUJIFILM
film, cameras, and Instax cameras
www.fujifilmusa.com

Golden Artist Colors, Inc.
acrylic paints, mediums
www.goldenpaints.com

Jacquard Products
textile and paper art supplies
www.jacquardproducts.com

Jerry's Artarama
art and craft supplies
www.jerrysartarama.com

JetPens
online Japanese pen and stationery store
www.JetPens.com

Liquitex Artist Materials
acrylic paints, mediums
www.liquitex.com

MisterArt.com
art and craft supplies
www.misterart.com

Moleskine Srl
journals
www.moleskine.com

Pentel of America, Ltd.
pens, markers
www.pentel.com

Polaroid
Polaroid PoGo printer and instant digital cameras
www.polaroid.com

Royal Talens
Rembrandt and Amsterdam/Van Gogh paints and pencils
www.talens.com

Sakura Color Products of America, Inc.
specialty pens, markers, and watercolors
www.sakuraofamerica.com

Staedtler, Inc.
paints, pens, watercolor crayons, and pencils
www.staedtler.com

Strathmore Artist Papers
paper and spiral-bound journals
www.strathmoreartist.com

Tsukineko, LLC.
rubber stamp pads
www.tsukineko.com

INSPIRATIONAL BOOKS AND LINKS

Traci Bunkers
Print & Stamp Lab (Quarry Books, 2010)
www.TraciBunkers.com

Julia Cameron
The Artist's Way (Tarcher, 2002)
www.theartistsway.com

Lucia Capacchione
The Creative Journal (New Page Books, 2001)
and *The Power of Your Other Hand* (New Page Books, 2001)
www.luciac.com

Mike Dooley
Notes from the Universe (Atria Books/Beyond Words, 2007)
www.tut.com

Louise Hay
You Can Heal Your Life (Hay House, 1984)
www.louisehay.com

Karen Michel
The Complete Guide to Altered Imagery (Quarry Books, 2005)
www.karenmichel.com

ABOUT THE AUTHOR

Traci Bunkers is a passionate and quirky self-employed mixed-media and fiber artist living in Lawrence, Kansas. "I love rusty things, glitter glue, old books to cut up, and cheap cameras. I'm smiling when my hands are dirty with paint or when I've altered a camera or something to use as a printing tool. It means I'm doing what I love—making art and doing things with my hands. Lucky for me, I do what I love for a living." For this self-proclaimed love child of MacGyver, making her own books and art journaling has been a longtime passion. She always feels better after getting her art on by slapping some paint down and working in her journal. Through her one-woman business, Bonkers Handmade Originals, she sells her nifty creations such as hand-dyed spinning fibers and yarns, original rubber stamps, handmade books, kits, and original artwork. She also creates an artzine called *Tub Legs*, designs knitwear, and is a knitting, spinning, and crochet technical editor. She has been teaching workshops across the United States since the early '90s and has branched out into online workshops. Her visual journal pages, artwork, and knit designs have been published in numerous books and magazines, and this is her second book. To learn more about her work, visit her website at www.TraciBunkers.com.

ACKNOWLEDGMENTS

I want to thank my friend and agent, Neil Salkind, for his support and for again helping to bring my dream to fruition. A mighty big thanks to my soul sister, Juliana Coles. Meeting her many years ago catapulted my visual journaling. Over the years she has introduced me not only to baby wipes, but to many books and authors, including the work of Lucia Capacchione, that have helped shape me as an artist and also as a person. Her support and presence in my life are a blessing. I really want to thank my editor, Mary Ann Hall, and the crew at Quarry Books for believing that I really could create this book and also film myself and shoot the pictures while doing it. Thanks to all of my workshop organizers, students, and followers over the years. Last but not least, thanks to my pets for their unconditional love (especially Ruby) and for putting up with my crazy work schedule (not that they really had a choice).

Special thanks to Sakura Color Products of America and JetPens for generously supplying some of the pens I used in creating this book.